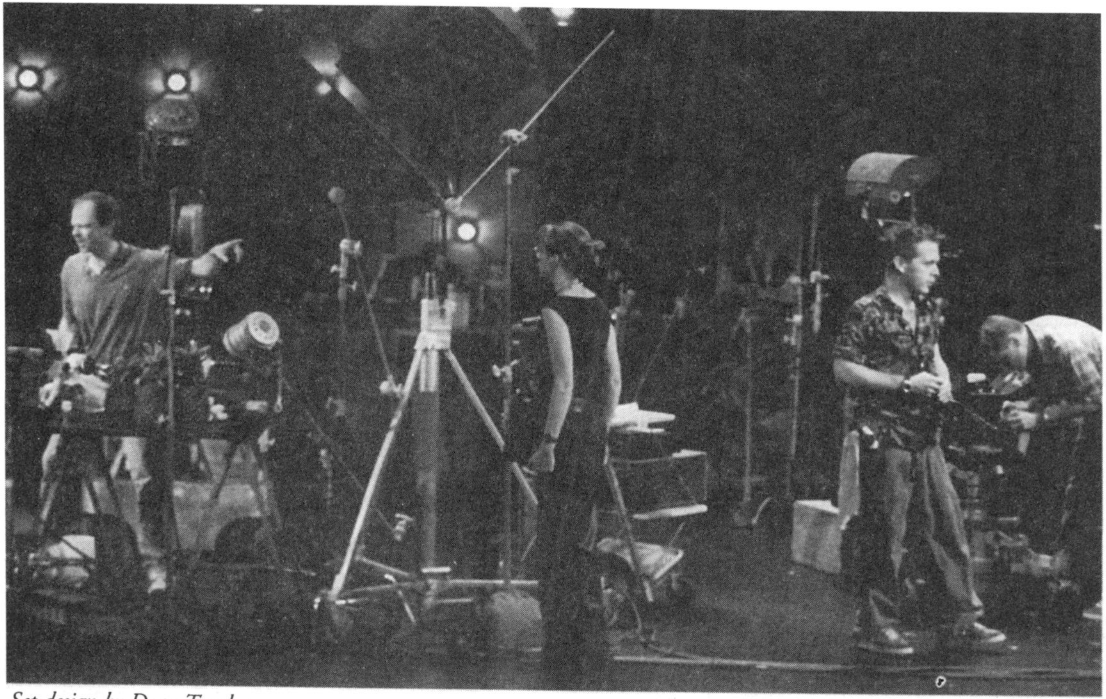

Set design by Dean Taucher

A scene from the New York production of *Tabletop*.

Photo by Carol Rosegg

TABLETOP

BY ROB ACKERMAN

★

DRAMATISTS
PLAY SERVICE
INC.

TABLETOP
Copyright © 2001, Rob Ackerman

All Rights Reserved

SPECIAL NOTE

This play is for A.R. Gurney.

AUTHOR'S NOTE

I have provided a description of the workplace that evolved for this play's first production. While it is important that real work be done throughout the action, the details of that work will vary with each staging. Please think of the set description as a list of ingredients, not a recipe.

Speaking of recipes, to create a "thick pink liquid," we dissolved the cottony and granular inner contents of disposable diapers in water, thinned that to a "slurpy" consistency and then puréed it in a blender to a pourable smoothness, adding a few drops of red food coloring and a dash of shaving cream. For the "swirl," we mixed food coloring into shaving cream and then squeezed it out of a pastry bag into the classic "Dairy Queen" shape.

There are two kinds of video used in the play. The "Chicago Demo Reel" consists of edited clips from polished commercials. I suggest you contact an actual tabletop director and ask for credited permission to use a couple of showy "spec spots." Appeal to directorial vanity. That's what we did.

"Ron's pour" or the "playback" should be recorded on your production's tabletop set using a home video camera. First, decide on the tabletop itself. Then come up with an arrangement of real and/or fake fruit (I suggest using as much fake stuff as possible) and let the actors rehearse the scenes involving the disassembling and assembling of the whole structure. Once you settle on a fruit landscape and the placement and design of the "hero cup," you can schedule your own simple video shoot. We asked a video expert to come in with his tripod and recording deck. He was able to achieve a slow motion effect and he even added "crosshairs" to simulate the "look" of a real video assist camera. There's computer software out there for just this purpose. Also, remember to make a backup of each videotape, just in case. In performance, both clips were cued and controlled from the stage manager's booth.

Finally, the events of the play occur in real time and gather momentum without an intermission. However, if one hundred uninterrupted minutes seems too extreme, the place you might pause would be after the crew files out to go to the loading dock. The second act would then begin with Dave returning to make his phone call.

TABLETOP was produced by The Working Theatre (Robert Arcaro, Artistic Director; Mark Plesent, Producing Director) in New York City on July 11, 2000. It was directed by Connie Grappo. The set design was by Dean Taucher; the lighting design was by Jack Mehler; the costume design was by Ilona Somogyi; the production manager was Allan Kerr; the stage manager was Neveen Mahmoud; and the assistant stage manager was Janine L. Pangburn. The cast was as follows:

OSCAR	Harvy Blanks
RON	Jeremy Webb
JEFFREY	Dean Nolen
DAVE	Jack Koenig
ANDREA	Elizabeth Hanly Rice
MARCUS	Rob Bartlett

TABLETOP was subsequently produced by Amy Danis, Dr. Richard Firestone, Joan D. Firestone, Mark Johannes, Ellen M. Krass in association with Karen Davidov at the American Place Theatre (Wynn Handman, Artistic Director; Carl H. Jaynes, General Manager) in New York City on October 31, 2000. It was directed by Connie Grappo. The set design was by Dean Taucher; the lighting design was by Jack Mehler; the costume design was by Ilona Somogyi; the general manager was Denise Cooper; and the production stage manager was Donald Fried. The cast was as follows:

OSCAR	Harvy Blanks
RON	Jeremy Webb
JEFFREY	Dean Nolen
DAVE	Jack Koenig
ANDREA	Elizabeth Hanly Rice
MARCUS	Rob Bartlett

CHARACTERS

RON — studio manager

OSCAR — gaffer, grip, and video operator

JEFFREY — property master

DAVE — assistant cameraman

ANDREA — producer and assistant director

MARCUS — director/cameraman and company owner

PLACE

The play takes place in the Manhattan studio of Marcus Gordon, a loft specially outfitted to film product shots for television commercials.

The studio itself should feel raw and industrial. Walls, ceilings and floors have been painted matte black. Upstage, workbenches and shelves hold bins of hardware, power tools and supplies. There's also a kitchen area up center with a refrigerator, sink and countertop. A gray steel bull switch, dimmer and phone/intercom have been mounted to a cement support column. Lighting and grip equipment line the wall stage left and a worktable there contains an open tool kit and other paraphernalia.

On a diagonal stage right, three steps lead up to a wood-paneled and carpeted walkway with a door leading off to an executive suite. Below the walkway is a "client area" with a couch and coffee table. By the downstage right wall, there's a small "craft service" table with snacks, drinks and cookies, and above it hangs a color video monitor, viewable from the stage and the audience.

A video playback deck and small monitor sit on a cart down left. Adhesive tapes, spray bottles and paper towels top a low rolling prop table down right. Dead center, a massive black high-speed camera looms from a dolly. The camera points at a "set," surrounded by lights and stands, which consists merely of a small square tabletop.

TIME

The time is a Monday around now.

TABLETOP

The stage is dimly lit by clip lights in the workshop, decorative lamps in the kitchen, and a glow from the frosted windows of the executive suite. Oscar, an African-American veteran gaffer in his early fifties, wears clean jeans and an equipment rental company's tee shirt. He enters ahead of Ron, carrying a takeout food container and a tabloid newspaper, tosses out his finished lunch, and sits on a plywood "apple box" near the set to read. Ron, the studio manager, handles the menial and thankless tasks that keep this place running. In his twenties, with orange hair, creative flair and irrepressible energy, he tags along behind Oscar holding a pile of mail which includes a cardboard FedEx envelope.

RON. ... I know this. I've learned this. With stuff like this, you don't always do what you mean to do — it's not like a conscious thing ... *(Ron switches on the studio's "house lights" and, through the following, peruses the mail and busily tidies the stage.)* Alexander Calder didn't sit down and decide to invent the mobile. No. No way. His father was a sculptor, so he studied engineering, and learned about structure, and then he looked at a globe — this was in, like, 1932 — and he figured he could make some steel solar systems and dangle them from rods and wires, but his planets didn't turn out to be spherical or circular. He didn't even know what to call them 'til Marcel Duchamp said "mobiles," which is sort of a pun in French on movement and motivation. So, I mean, it wasn't like Calder was on a career track or anything. He was just working with what he liked. And that's all I want to do. I'm getting back to

what I did in day camp when it was all about strips of gloopy newspaper and smearing them onto a shiny balloon.

OSCAR. Ron.

RON. Yeah?

OSCAR. Simplify.

RON. You mean my — ?

OSCAR. Simplify. Sim … pli … fy.

RON. Oscar, I'm sorry, could you please elaborate?

OSCAR. You walk out on set and it's like there's three of you,
man. And you're all arguing with yourself and discussing with
yourself and on and on. And that's not the way to be. Look at me:
What do I say? When I'm settin' a stand and someone's in my way,
what do I say?

RON. Oscar, I am not you.

OSCAR. Do I say, "Beg your pardon"? Do I say, "Watch your
back"? Do I say, "Excuse me"?

RON. No.

OSCAR. I say, "MOVE!"

RON. I know that.

OSCAR. "MOVE!"

RON. I can't just say "MOVE."

OSCAR. Yes you can.

RON. I am not so assertive.

OSCAR. I'm not talkin' about what you are; I'm talkin' about
what you wanna be. Twenty years ago, I didn't know from nothin'.
I was workin' up at the Handi Stop baggin' Ring Dings and
Hostess Ho-Hos. I was nowhere, man. And then I get a call from
an old army buddy o' mine. Richie. Richie Rose. Tells me he's
workin' in the film business. And I'm thinkin' ol' Richie's Mister
Hollywood!

RON. He's doing tabletop?

OSCAR. Gets me a job over at Ampersand. And I'm in there
watchin' them shoot a bottle of Budweiser through twelve hundred pounds o' crushed ice and I'm thinking, hell, you know: This
ain't no film business. I don't know what it is, but it sure looks like
MONEY to me, you know what I'm sayin'?

RON. (Jiving.) Bread and butter.

OSCAR. And we're talkin' *premium* bread — Pepperidge Farm.

12

So I'm goin' aroun' playin' Production Assistant, pickin' up the soda cans, sortin' the cornflakes. Just like you.

RON. I hear you.

OSCAR. And then this cocky little crew-cut second electric comes over and tells me to run out and get some "zip cord." Tells me he needs fifty feet of "zip cord." Now, I don't know what "zip cord" is, but I'm hopin' my man at the hardware store's gonna help me out.

RON. Uh-oh.

OSCAR. And I get there and Mister-Ace-Servicestar-Plastic-Pen-Pouch-Name-Stitched-Over-The-Pocket-"Bob" — he ain't no help at all. And I come back with a hank o' cotton clothesline. Hey, crew cut, he coulda told me electric wire, but he was settin' me up. They always got to pick on somebody. *(Jeffrey and Dave hustle in, shedding their coats and shoulder bags. Jeffrey's the property master, a cocky professional craftsperson in jeans, polo shirt and industry-standard New Balance sneakers. Dave, assistant cameraman, looks a bit more refined in chinos and boating shoes. As Jeffrey straps on his tool belt, Ron turns his attention to opening the FedEx envelope, which contains a 3/4-inch videotape in a plastic case.)*

JEFFREY. *(In midconversation as he enters.)* No, man, I'm telling you, the guy's an animal. He does all this stuff you just don't do. He gangs up a dozen Six K Pars with no lenses. Three Twenty K's and a Ruby Seven. He gets so much light in there, he makes a red pepper transparent. He friggin' irradiates the sucker, goes totally nuclear.

OSCAR. Who you talkin'?

DAVE. One guess.

JEFFREY. Large midwestern city.

OSCAR. Chicago?

JEFFREY. *(Like he's the hottest thing ever.)* Worked with him last week.

OSCAR. Oh, did you?

DAVE. I heard he shoots three hundred frames at a twenty-two. God. I thought that was impossible.

JEFFREY. He *melted* a Corian countertop.

OSCAR. Damn.

JEFFREY. He turned it into soup. We're talking a whole different scale here. The gaffer told me he had a fifteen-thousand-dollar lighting bill for an insert shot.

DAVE. How's his footage? *(Ron has quietly inserted a tape into the $\frac{3}{4}$-inch deck, and now tabletop shots fade up on the color video screen.)*

JEFFREY. His what?

DAVE. How does his stuff look?

JEFFREY. *(Noticing the video.)* Check it out — this is his reel. *(Ron turns up the sound and they all turn to watch a beer commercial.)* Woo, look at that pour.

OSCAR. See that flare?

JEFFREY. Totally blows out the background.

OSCAR. It's burnin' up.

JEFFREY. You gotta wear welding glasses when you shoot this stuff. I'm telling you. It's all about the Epsom salts, man.

DAVE. I think it's all about the f-stop.

JEFFREY. Well, that too. *(A sparkling beverage spot begins.)* Check it out: one, two, three drops.

DAVE. That's underwater unilux.

OSCAR. Gotta be.

DAVE. See the strobes?

JEFFREY. Look at that vortex ... see those bubbles?

RON. They shot that in reverse.

JEFFREY. Obviously.

DAVE. Nice water work. *(Jeffrey turns off the monitor.)*

JEFFREY. *(To Ron.)* What're you doing with this?

RON. It came in the mail. Marcus must've requested it. I was curious.

OSCAR. Marcus is checkin' out the competition.

DAVE. The guy took Red Lobster. *(Jeffrey crosses to the video cart and ejects the tape from the deck.)*

JEFFREY. Shit.

DAVE. I heard he's bidding Burger King.

OSCAR. The man must be good.

JEFFREY. *(Shutting the tape into its plastic case and handing it to Ron.)* Ron, you're the studio manager. You make the coffee, you don't read the boss's mail. These are little rules for living.

RON. I was gonna put it back.

JEFFREY. Bury it. *(Ron puts the tape on the coffee table.)*

RON. Um, I'm not positive, but I'm pretty sure the guy's a hack.
JEFFREY. Says who?
RON. Says nobody, actually. Nobody would dare question such an obvious genius. I just have this feeling. It just seems to me it's pretty easy for this Chicago fellow to stand there and ask for *more* of everything. And it's cool, right? It's cool to do that. And it's expensive, which is also cool. It makes a good story. They all talk about you at lunch.
JEFFREY. Well, Ron, what would you do?
RON. I don't know, Jeffrey. I'm not so impressed by the big guns. That's not advertising.
JEFFREY. Oh, and what is advertising, according to you?
RON. Okay, in my opinion, a commercial — a thirty-second spot on TV — is the single most eloquent statement of our time. *(Oscar and Jeffrey laugh loudly.)* I swear to God, I'm serious. Movies, novels, sitcoms ... I mean, who has the patience? It's totally over for them. Now it's all like Nike and Pepsi and Monster Dot-Com.
JEFFREY. Well, I just hit my mute button.
RON. And I don't. *(Jeffrey picks up a little Igloo cooler.)*
JEFFREY. What's this?
RON. Nothing.
JEFFREY. Have you been workin' on the swirl?
OSCAR. He stayed straight through lunch.
JEFFREY. You tryin' to make me look bad?
RON. No. God no, Jeffrey. Not at all. This was just — I don't know — penance. Or whatever. I'm still experimenting. *(Jeffrey opens the cooler and lifts out a cup topped with a swirl of pink foam: You'd think he'd seen the Holy Grail.)*
JEFFREY. Mother of God.
OSCAR. Look at that.
DAVE. How did you do it?
OSCAR. He ain't tellin'.
RON. It's not perfect.
JEFFREY. No, Ron, it's good — it's very good.
RON. I still want to work on it.
JEFFREY. Don't. Don't touch it. He doesn't want you doing prop work. Don't be stupid. Just let me handle it, okay? *(Jeffrey returns the cup to the cooler and carefully closes the lid as Andrea enters. She's*

lean, aggressive and all-business, the mediator between the boss, clients and crew. In leather pants and filmy blouse, she uses both sexiness and sharpness to maximum advantage.)

ANDREA. *(Consulting her clipboard.)* Okay, we're in. Take off the tarp and have a hero ready. He says he's gonna shoot the rehearsal.

JEFFREY. Here we go, Ronnie boy, who loves you? *(Jeffrey and Ron take the four corners of a piece of plastic sheeting and lift it off the center stage tabletop to reveal a black square surface on sawhorses supporting an elaborate mountain of fresh fruit.)*

ANDREA. Jeffrey.

JEFFREY. We'll be fine.

ANDREA. I hope you have a plan.

JEFFREY. Do it 'til we get it right.

ANDREA. That's no good.

JEFFREY. This is trial and error.

ANDREA. No, Jeffrey. It's right or wrong. And we got nothing but wrong all morning.

JEFFREY. Is that what he's saying?

ANDREA. He's not happy.

JEFFREY. Shit.

ANDREA. It's just the first of two shots. I don't want you to make a career of this one. We've still gotta get to that swirl.

JEFFREY. I know.

ANDREA. Just give us a good strong pour. That's all we want. That's all we need. *(Andrea exits.)*

JEFFREY. Christ, it's cold.

RON. Andrea had me set the thermostat at sixty.

JEFFREY. That makes a lot of sense. Chill the fruit. Kill the crew.

RON. I'll hand you a hero.

JEFFREY. Just let me get a position first. *(Jeffrey plants himself in front of the tangle of lighting and grip equipment and checks a mark at the top of the arrangement of fruit. He reaches back as Ron hands him a perfect plastic cup. He places the cup atop the fruit and adjusts the orientation of the logo.)*

OSCAR. *(Taking Dave aside.)* You got that commitment letter?

DAVE. Yes, it's in the folder.

OSCAR. So what do we do?

DAVE. Nothing. It has some instructions on the cover page. Sign it, fax it, order a wire transfer …

OSCAR. Let's do it.

DAVE. I want to go over it one more time.

OSCAR. Come on, man, you've gone over it *fifty* times. *(Jeffrey crosses to the prop table and takes charge as Ron reaches into a large cooler for a Ziploc pouch full of pink liquid.)*

JEFFREY. Okay, here's how I want to work: I'm gonna prep the liquid. I'm gonna climb the ladder. I'm gonna do the pour. *(Ron spills a bit of liquid and Jeffrey takes the Ziploc pouch out of his hands.)* All you've gotta do is keep things clean. *(Jeffrey watches Ron tear off some paper towels and drop to his hands and knees to wipe up his mess.)* I know you want to get in there, Ron; I know you want to be involved. But this is not the time. We need to keep you out of the way.

RON. I'm not in the way. *(Jeffrey pours the liquid into a bowl and whips it with a wire whisk.)*

JEFFREY. You ever think of going freelance, Ron?

RON. There's no work.

JEFFREY. I'm just saying —

RON. Oscar says it's as slow as he's seen it.

JEFFREY. There's always something.

RON. Not in tabletop.

JEFFREY. Listen to me. You did a nice job on that swirl. And I know you want to show him. But you're not the prop guy here. That's my world. *(Marcus, a big man with a big ego, strides in. As director, he's king, and this room is his realm. Andrea pushes the workers like pawns before him.)*

MARCUS. Here we go.

ANDREA. Settle in, everyone. Oscar, get a frame count. Jeffrey?

JEFFREY. Standing by.

DAVE. Three hundred and sixty frames.

OSCAR. Watch your eyes. *(Oscar slams a steel lever on a heavy-duty electrical box, a "bull switch." Blindingly bright tungsten lamps illuminate the arrangement of fruit. Jeffrey takes a pitcher to the top of a four-step ladder and prepares to pour pink liquid into the plastic cup. Marcus goes right to work.)*

MARCUS. Dolly me in. C'mon, don't make me wait. Are we on our mark?

OSCAR. Where we were.

DAVE. Locked and loaded.

MARCUS. What's that reading?

DAVE. Eight eleven on the key.

MARCUS. Back off the fill.

OSCAR. On the fill.

MARCUS. Hold that. Good. That's good.

ANDREA. How's the fruit?

JEFFREY. The fruit's fine.

MARCUS. Spritz the grapes.

RON. Right away.

JEFFREY. Easy.

RON. *(Reaching through the clutter of stands.)* Spritzing.

MARCUS. The grapes. Not the lemon. Not the fuckin' lemon.

RON. I've got a Q-tip.

MARCUS. Jesus.

ANDREA. Jeffrey?

JEFFREY. Standing by.

MARCUS. Listen, Jeffrey. You saw what I want. That shape that I showed you.

JEFFREY. Yes, sir.

MARCUS. You gonna give me that?

JEFFREY. I got it.

MARCUS. I'm talkin' thick.

JEFFREY. Very good.

MARCUS. Thick.

JEFFREY. I hear you.

MARCUS. Thick, Jeffrey.

JEFFREY. Yes, sir.

MARCUS. Let's do it.

ANDREA. Let's go.

MARCUS. Stop down.

DAVE. Stopping down.

ANDREA. Roll tape.

OSCAR. Tape speed.

ANDREA. Camera. *(The photosonics camera revs up to a loud and annoying whine.)*

DAVE. *(Shouting above the noise of the camera.)* SPEED! *(Jeffrey*

pours thick pink liquid into the cup, carefully finishing without spilling a drop.)
MARCUS. And, CUT!
ANDREA. Save the lights. Playback.
MARCUS. What do you think? *(Oscar shuts off the bull switch.)*
JEFFREY. It felt good.
MARCUS. Yeah?
JEFFREY. Yeah.
OSCAR. *(At the video deck.)* Two hundred frames.
MARCUS. *(Watching playback.)* Andrea ...
ANDREA. Yeah.
MARCUS. You see that?
ANDREA. It's right on the crosshairs.
MARCUS. Freeze it there. It's wimpy, Andrea.
ANDREA. It's accurate.
MARCUS. It's not what I want.
ANDREA. He showed you.
MARCUS. What'd I say?
ANDREA. He heard you.
MARCUS. I said thick. It's gotta have that muscle. It's gotta have that twist. Right? Right in there. You wanna watch it again?
ANDREA. There's no need.
MARCUS. So go on. Get it right. It can't be that hard.
ANDREA. Reset.
MARCUS. How long?
JEFFREY. Five minutes.
ANDREA. Five minutes. *(Oscar throws the bull switch, restores normal room lighting, and Marcus walks out.)*
JEFFREY. This is bullshit.
ANDREA. It's this client.
JEFFREY. I swear, I'm not sure if this shot is even possible.
ANDREA. They got it in Chicago.
JEFFREY. It was a different liquid. A different viscosity. There's physics to this, Andrea.
ANDREA. Why don't you put Ron on it?
JEFFREY. Oh no way.
ANDREA. He might just get lucky.
JEFFREY. Yeah. Sure. Right.

ANDREA. You working on the swirl?

JEFFREY. What?

ANDREA. We need a new hero.

JEFFREY. I kept them all in the freezer.

ANDREA. What you had on Friday?

JEFFREY. They were fine.

ANDREA. They were acceptable.

JEFFREY. *(Making a decision.)* I might have something better.

ANDREA. Yeah?

JEFFREY. I did a little work during lunch.

ANDREA. You got something I can show him?

JEFFREY. I hope so.

ANDREA. Did you talk to Ron?

JEFFREY. Why?

ANDREA. He told me he had an idea.

JEFFREY. Andrea, you know the rule: If it's Ron, it's wrong.

ANDREA. You saw what he did?

JEFFREY. I have to tweak it.

ANDREA. So go over there and do a dumb show, Jeffrey. And then we can say that you solved the swirl. I don't really care how you want to play this, but I've got two shots to get here and frankly I'm beginning to worry.

JEFFREY. Ron.

RON. Yeah.

JEFFREY. You're on.

RON. On what?

JEFFREY. The pour.

RON. You're kidding.

ANDREA. You know what we want?

RON. Yeah. Sure. I mean, yes. I mean … yes. I do. *(Jeffrey crosses to the prop table. Ron takes the pitcher of pink liquid and starts practicing. Andrea opens her clipboard and moves to the video monitor, brushing by Oscar.)*

ANDREA. I need a script note.

OSCAR. Hey, careful, baby.

ANDREA. Sorry.

OSCAR. You can't just bump up against a man like that.

ANDREA. Take it easy.

OSCAR. Ain't ever easy ...

ANDREA. Six baker: Ron on the pour. *(Marcus enters and sees Andrea coaching Ron.)*

ANDREA. Ron, you're going on "speed." Okay? On "speed."

RON. On "speed."

MARCUS. Andrea.

ANDREA. *(Crossing to Marcus.)* We're ready.

MARCUS. What're you doing?

ANDREA. I am doing my job.

MARCUS. I can't trust that fuckin' kid.

ANDREA. So trust me. We need to mix things up. Jerry's gonna call and ask what we've got. *(Marcus protests. He and Andrea argue sotto voce. Marcus gives up and crosses to camera, taking a sip from his stainless steel mug.)*

MARCUS. What's this coffee?

ANDREA. What about it?

MARCUS. Tastes like candy.

RON. That's the chicory.

ANDREA. That's the what?

RON. Cuts the bitterness.

ANDREA. I can send someone out.

RON. I've got a bag of Sumatra in the freezer. Just the beans, I mean. I'd have to get out the grinder.

MARCUS. Can we shoot this?

ANDREA. How's the surface?

MARCUS. It's fine. It's fine. I wanna go.

ANDREA. On the lights.

MARCUS. Hold on. *(To Ron.)* Now, listen. Listen to me. I want some thickness here. I want to see some muscle here. I want it to fill the frame.

RON. Actually, I did practice a bit after we left on Friday and I think that by pouring out of the side of the pitcher, I was able to achieve some of that twisting turbulence that you saw in the reference shot.

MARCUS. Andrea.

ANDREA. Lights. *(Oscar throws the bull switch.)*

MARCUS. Stop down.

DAVE. Stopping down.

ANDREA. Oscar?

OSCAR. Standing by.

ANDREA. Ron?

RON. Standing by.

ANDREA. Roll video.

OSCAR. Tape speed.

ANDREA. Camera. *(The photosonics camera revs to its roar.)*

DAVE. SPEED! *(Ron extends his wrist like a matador and pours the pink liquid from an impressive height above the cup. As he attempts to finish with a flourish, the cup overflows and Ron slops liquid onto the fruit.)*

ANDREA. CUT!

MARCUS. FUCKING CHRIST!

RON. I'm sorry.

MARCUS. FUCKING FUCKING CHRIST!

RON. Sorry.

JEFFREY. Don't apologize.

MARCUS. Who is this guy?

JEFFREY. Bring me the bucket.

MARCUS. Who in the fuck does he think he is?

RON. I tried to give it that twist.

JEFFREY. Don't defend yourself.

MARCUS. You were SHIT. You were SHIT is what you were. You spilled SHIT all over six hours of my hard work.

RON. I'm sorry.

MARCUS. You think I do this for SPORT?

RON. No.

MARCUS. You had a chance, you fuck. The fucking girl gave you a chance. And now LOOK what you FUCKING DID!!!

ANDREA. Kill the lights.

OSCAR. Killing. *(Oscar throws the bull switch.)*

MARCUS. JEFFREY!

JEFFREY. Yes, Marcus.

MARCUS. I want YOU on standby. I want YOU on every take. You got that?

JEFFREY. Got it.

MARCUS. I want YOU on the prep, YOU on the pour, YOU on the cleanup, YOU on the marks, YOU on every goddamn thing. This guy just hands you what you need. He stands there and hands you what you need. He does not get near my set. *(Wheeling on Ron.)* You are dangerous. You are fucking dangerous, kid. You could fuck up a one-car funeral. What are you, standin' there, teeth in your mouth? Come on, do something! Rip some paper towels! Jesus fuck! Nice work, Andrea.

ANDREA. I need to —

MARCUS. Not now.

ANDREA. Marcus —

MARCUS. NOT NOW! *(Marcus storms out, slamming the upstage door.)*

OSCAR. Does he wanna see playback?

ANDREA. How long?

JEFFREY. Maybe an hour.

ANDREA. Twenty minutes.

JEFFREY. No chance.

RON. I'll help.

JEFFREY. No thank you.

OSCAR. Let him help.

JEFFREY. He's not in my category.

OSCAR. Who cares?

ANDREA. Listen. Now, listen. I want the Mitchell on the Spider for the second shot. This thing comes apart and goes back together in less than twenty minutes. And everybody works. Nobody bickers. Got it?

DAVE. Got it.

JEFFREY. Got it.

ANDREA. Good. *(Andrea exits upstage.)*

DAVE. Let's get these grip stands out of our way.

OSCAR. I'm on that.

JEFFREY. We need more paper towels. *(Jeffrey crosses to his table. Oscar starts clearing away equipment. Dave goes to get a Spider dolly for the "second camera setup," which he and Oscar assemble stage left for the next half hour.)*

OSCAR. Ron.

RON. Yeah.

OSCAR. Don't let him rattle you.

JEFFREY. All right. Here we go. We start at the back. I mark each piece in grease pencil, and you dip it in the bucket here.

23

RON. Okay.

JEFFREY. Then you dry it with a piece of paper towel. And then you take every berry, every banana, and you put it on the prop table in exactly the same position. You build the same setup over there. Then I clean the surface — no Bestine, just Windex, 'cause we gotta keep our marks. And I put the whole thing back together, piece by piece, exactly the same way, and check it to the Polaroids.

RON. Fine.

JEFFREY. It's a beautiful thing. It's stupid, but it's beautiful. The stupid way is the best way. *(Reaching for the first piece of fruit.)* Here we go. Upstage. Camera left. The Bartlett pear. Stem at eleven o'clock. Thirty-degree tilt. With this little rounded reddish section facing forward. *(Oscar and Dave prepare the Spider dolly.)*

DAVE. He wants the geared head.

OSCAR. Is that what he said?

DAVE. That's what he had.

OSCAR. He could change his mind.

DAVE. You want to go back there and ask him?

OSCAR. Funny, Dave. Yeah. Real funny.

RON. Jeffrey. I just have to tell you. I'm not worried.

JEFFREY. In the bucket.

RON. I know.

JEFFREY. Carefully.

RON. I know.

JEFFREY. I mean it.

DAVE. *(Struggling with a dolly leg.)* Where's that can of WD?

RON. I'm sorry, guys, I took it.

OSCAR. Ron, don't worry —

JEFFREY. I want him to worry.

RON. I'm perfectly capable of doing this pour.

JEFFREY. You made a mess, Ron.

RON. Yeah, but it was a *great* mess! It was, Jeffrey. I swear, sometimes I think Marcus is, like, scared of me or something.

JEFFREY. Ron, I really doubt it, okay?

RON. He said I'm dangerous.

JEFFREY. You're an entry-level employee. Marcus makes ten grand a day. Get over yourself. *(Ron drops an apple. It rolls across the floor.)*

RON. Oh no. *(Andrea enters from the office, eyes down on her clipboard. She sees Ron and Jeffrey frozen there and the two of them resume work. Andrea heads upstage to the kitchen area. Through the following, she prepares a salad.)*

JEFFREY. *(Like a bank robber instructing the teller.)* No sudden moves. Quietly, now. Quietly. Go over and get the apple. *(Ron does as he's told.)* Hold it in both hands. Good. Now take it to the table and check the damage. Listen to me, Ron. If the apple is bruised or cut in any way, and I think it is, I want you to just set it aside. *(Ron scrutinizes the apple and then places it "aside" on top of three stacked rolls of tape.)* Good. Now go in the back and go through all our hero apples and select the most similar one. Do you understand? *(Ron nods, heads upstage and then sheepishly circles back to Jeffrey.)* Go. *(Ron stands there.)* Go, Ron. *(Ron won't budge.)* Go.

RON. There aren't any apples.

JEFFREY. We got six cases.

RON. I sent them to the soup kitchen.

JEFFREY. No! No! Not the heros.

RON. He said we were wrapped.

JEFFREY. Goddamn it!

RON. It's just this little scuff. Why don't we just clock it? You won't even see the scar.

JEFFREY. Put it back. Just put the apple back. Okay?

RON. You want me to clock it?

JEFFREY. Where it was. Put it back where it was. Listen, Ron, no one has to know about this.

RON. But —

JEFFREY. I know you want to be a good boy. I know you want to do the right thing and be honest, but just forget it. Forget it ever happened.

RON. He'll notice.

JEFFREY. He won't. I'm telling you. Forget it. *(Andrea passes them, pauses and then exits.)*

RON. You sure you don't want to clock it just the tiniest bit?

JEFFREY. Ron.

RON. What?

JEFFREY. Stop thinking.

RON. I'm not thinking.

JEFFREY. Two hands.

RON. I got it.

JEFFREY. Take it with two hands.

RON. Marcus doesn't like me. He never liked me. He just used to hide it better.

JEFFREY. He doesn't have to like you; he gives you a paycheck and petty cash.

RON. You know, I don't really care who pours the pink stuff.

JEFFREY. Take the grapes.

RON. Let me just say this for a second, okay?

JEFFREY. Would you please be careful?

RON. I have been here for two years. And I haven't missed one shoot day, okay? I missed my uncle's funeral, my parents' anniversary, but not one shoot day. And he's got the nerve to turn to you and say, "Who is this guy?" Like I'm some bum who walked in off the street.

JEFFREY. Ron, we all know you do a good job.

RON. We do?

JEFFREY. Except when you don't.

RON. And when's that?

JEFFREY. When you wanna think about everything.

RON. Oh. Okay. Like when you told me to decapitate ten dozen baby roses, and I just mentioned that I could see how sick that was?

JEFFREY. Perfect example.

RON. Okay, Jeffrey, what's a rose supposed to do?

JEFFREY. I don't know.

RON. What? Tell me. What? Dave? Oscar? It blooms. It blossoms. A rose reveals itself over time. It has a gesture and a fragrance. So when I cut those baby roses, I will admit that something about it felt wrong to me. But we needed those petals to put them on a conveyor belt to drop them on a package to market a moisturizer to all the women who aren't quite as moist as they wish they could be.

JEFFREY. You see what I mean?

RON. So I think too much. So what? Who cares?

JEFFREY. All of us, I believe, as a matter of fact —

RON. I can think and do my job.

JEFFREY. Can you *not* think and do your job?

RON. I don't know.

26

JEFFREY. Ron, what do you want?

RON. Less abuse. Okay? I want less abuse.

JEFFREY. How 'bout a hug?

RON. Go to hell.

OSCAR. I hate reshoots. There's nothin' worse. We shouldn't even be here. Skeleton stinkin' crew. You ever seen such a thing? I'm doing video damn playback. Bad enough he doesn't hire a grip. I'm the gaffer, I'm the grip, I'm on video. Might as well clean the restrooms. Am I right, Ron? Man's gonna have me cleanin' the restrooms. *(Ron grabs the bucket and exits. Jeffrey crosses to the kitchen sink to wash a wooden support for the fruit. Oscar approaches Dave.)* Dave, what's goin' on, man?

DAVE. Nothing.

OSCAR. Come on, now. I'm not stupid. You're backin' out on me.

DAVE. No.

OSCAR. Dave, listen. Whatever it is, just think about it. Think about that bric-a-brac on the ceiling and the sawdust on the floor and sittin' outside on a pair o' nice lounge chairs sippin' hot cider and sayin' good mornin'. It's a general store, man, and you and me, we're the generals!

DAVE. I'm a jerk.

OSCAR. No, you're not.

DAVE. I know how much this means to you, Oscar.

OSCAR. It's a very good deal.

DAVE. I know. I know. It's nothing to do with the deal.

OSCAR. What?

DAVE. You remember that thing at the New York Hilton?

OSCAR. Show Biz Expo?

DAVE. Well, I went. And Panavision had this little booth to show off their unusual lenses. And there was this beautiful person there whose job was to demonstrate the Frazier System and ... it's no big thing, but it might get to be a bigger thing ... I think. I hope ...

OSCAR. It's about damn time, my brother. That's what you needed was a good woman. What's her name? *(Ron enters and goes right back to work.)*

DAVE. No, but, the thing is ... what I'm thinking is ... it might get to be too much if I'm starting this store out in Jersey and spending all my weekends on Cape Cod.

27

OSCAR. Cape Cod?

JEFFREY. Wait a minute.

RON. What?

JEFFREY. I had Fun-tak. This is butyl. You're using butyl.

RON. No it's not. It's a hybrid. It's a mix of Fun-tak and that auto glass adhesive that comes in a coil.

JEFFREY. And it works?

RON. It's great. It's stronger. It's stickier. And it's black, so if, God forbid, we make a mistake, it won't show up.

OSCAR. Dave, I'm happy for you.

DAVE. Well, it's not —

OSCAR. No, I am. I'm happy about all that. Cape Cod. Whatever. But we made an agreement ...

DAVE. A verbal agreement.

OSCAR. Don't you tell me that. It was a done deal. You got the piece of paper to prove it.

DAVE. Well, at least Marcus will be happy.

OSCAR. Yeah, and what'll I be? What about that? *(Dave retreats, exiting up left.)* Dave!

ANDREA. What's the matter?

OSCAR. Dave's backing out on me.

ANDREA. I thought you two had a letter of agreement.

OSCAR. Oh, sure, he has it. He's not gonna sign it. He got a new girlfriend.

ANDREA. Oh, Oscar, that's so lame.

OSCAR. It's easy for him, you know, he can do her and be doin' me too.

ANDREA. Maybe I could help you with this ...

OSCAR. What?

ANDREA. ... get Marcus to come in as a silent partner.

OSCAR. You got to be kiddin'. He was kickin' the chairs. He hated the damn idea.

ANDREA. No, no, Oscar, I think I could convince him.

OSCAR. What's he want?

ANDREA. Nothing. He likes you. He respects you. *(Off a look from Oscar.)* He wants to keep you happy, okay? And if you'd be willing to be there for us, then we can be there for you. We get you your store and you work on our jobs.

OSCAR. Just your jobs?

ANDREA. When we need you, we don't want you booked with the man up the street. You're our first call, Oscar. You know that.

OSCAR. I'm gonna have to think about it.

ANDREA. Take your time. There's no pressure. You're family here. Marcus feels comfortable with you. And that's worth a lot. I could probably write you a check this afternoon.

OSCAR. Thank you, Andrea.

ANDREA. It's our pleasure.

OSCAR. Mmm. *(Andrea crosses left.)*

ANDREA. Oh. Hey. Listen, Marcus was asking about this stage box.

OSCAR. What about it?

ANDREA. He asked if you could rewire it.

OSCAR. That porcelain piece of crap? He should throw it away. The thing's garbage.

ANDREA. That's not what he thinks.

OSCAR. Andrea, I'm a union technician. I fill out a time card just like everybody else. I'm not the man's janitor. *(Marcus enters from up right, heads down left, and sees the setup that Dave and Oscar have been assembling with a geared camera head on top.)*

MARCUS. Gimme the Ceco over here.

OSCAR. This is what you had on Friday.

MARCUS. Fuck Friday. This isn't fuckin' Friday. Gimme the fuckin' friction head.

OSCAR. Yes, sir.

MARCUS. Oscar, she show you that stage box? You see that? You see what I gotta deal with?

OSCAR. I could take a look.

MARCUS. Crack it open. Fix it for me, Oscar. I need some decent equipment.

OSCAR. Very good, sir. *(A look between Oscar and Andrea.)*

MARCUS. *(On his way out.)* I want you to price out that pizza job. New and non-new boxes, three cheese pulls, and a bite-and-smile. Two twelves and some O.T. ... *(Marcus and Andrea exit.)*

RON. Oh God, not pizza again.

OSCAR. *(To Dave, with an edge.)* He wants the Ceco.

JEFFREY. Ron, we do the jobs because we do the jobs; we're not here to make things interesting for you.

OSCAR. Don't disrespect him.

JEFFREY. I'm not dissing him, Oscar. I'm teaching him. He keeps making the same mistakes.

DAVE. And you don't make mistakes?

JEFFREY. Dave ... you look so nice in that shirt — does it come in any heterosexual colors? *(Andrea enters.)*

ANDREA. Dave, what are you doing?

RON. He's loafing. That's what we do when you're not around. We loaf.

ANDREA. I'm talking about my e-mail.

DAVE. I figured.

ANDREA. I'm right here.

DAVE. I thought it might be easier.

ANDREA. I wouldn't wanna hear it? I don't wanna hear it. That's this Friday. This week. That leaves me three days.

DAVE. Four.

ANDREA. Not a lot of notice.

DAVE. I said I'd replace myself.

ANDREA. It's a shoot day, Dave. You don't replace yourself on shoot days. Not around here.

DAVE. I'm sorry, Andrea.

ANDREA. We won't go long. It's a candy bar break. Cookie Crunch.

DAVE. Yes, I remember.

ANDREA. So give us the day.

DAVE. That's not possible.

ANDREA. We had you on *hold.*

DAVE. I'm not available.

ANDREA. You're sure, Dave?

DAVE. Positive.

ANDREA. I'll tell him. *(Andrea walks out.)*

OSCAR. What is up with everyone?

RON. Marcus is shit and we are downhill.

DAVE. And the client's not here.

JEFFREY. Which is a good thing.

RON. I don't know. Having the client here is like a dysfunctional family having a guest at dinner. At least everyone behaves.

OSCAR. Hand me that grip arm.
RON. I got it. *(Andrea returns.)*
ANDREA. How's it looking?
JEFFREY. I'm having some trouble with the grapes.
ANDREA. Can you put something underneath?
JEFFREY. You'll see it.
ANDREA. How'd you have it before?
RON. You can't just expect it to turn out the same.
JEFFREY. May I speak with you a second? *(Taking Andrea aside.)*
I don't want Ron in my rice bowl.
ANDREA. There's too much to do.
JEFFREY. He just makes it harder.
ANDREA. Forget it. You're not gonna stand up top with your
plastic pitcher and then hurry down and spritz the grapes and
wipe the Formica. I'm not running a Chinese fire drill.
JEFFREY. I'd be better off —
ANDREA. I said no. Ron stays on standby. That's the last I want
to hear about it. *(Marcus enters.)*
MARCUS. How we doin'?
ANDREA. Not there yet — how long, Jeffrey? *(Marcus spots the
videotape from Chicago among the papers on the coffee table.)*
MARCUS. What is this?
ANDREA. Oh my God ...
JEFFREY. Ron.
MARCUS. What the fuck is this?
ANDREA. It's junk mail.
MARCUS. What's it doing on my table? In my studio? Who put
this here?
RON. I ... *(Jeffrey holds up a hand, silencing Ron.)*
MARCUS. You believe this? You fucking believe this shit? "State
of the art ... next generation ... the news you need to hear ... the
most talked-about tabletop production company in the world"!
Well, fuck me up the ass!
ANDREA. Throw it out. Go on. Burn it.
MARCUS. No, no, no. We should spend some time with this.
Read all about the new god of the industry from the Land of
Lincoln.
JEFFREY. He's just the flavor of the month.

31

MARCUS. No, he's good. He's very good. I want to ask you why.

ANDREA. Don't go there.

MARCUS. I'll tell you. I'll tell you why. Because of me. He's like me. But better.

ANDREA. So feel flattered.

MARCUS. I do. I am. I am so flattered I wanna fly out to Chicago, walk into his prissy little brick and brushed aluminum office, and piss in his mouth. *(Opening the case.)* Look at this. He has a little history of tabletop here. As if he has any idea. He's lookin' at the forest. I saw the fuckin' acorns.

JEFFREY. What a joke.

MARCUS. People used to knock off their product shots in ten minutes at the end of the day. Really. I'm serious. And then someone finally figured out that you couldn't even read the name on the bag of donuts. And all of a sudden, all of the advertising agencies, they all saw the same thing. They saw that these guys they were hiring to shoot their TV commercials, none of them gave a flying fuck about shooting product. They hardly even knew what a product shot was. So the agencies got smart and went looking for photographers. Studio still-life photographers. Someroff, Ficalora, Elbert. And me.

RON. You solved all their problems.

MARCUS. We knew what to do. We knew lighting, composition, appetite appeal.

ANDREA. Marcus, this isn't the time.

MARCUS. These guys gotta hear this. It's a fact. Right now, if you're working in advertising, there's only one thing that matters: Carl Havens.

ANDREA. Oh, come on.

MARCUS. People talk. They're on the phone all day. And all they hear is Havens botched the product shots on Nabisco.

ANDREA. It wasn't even his fault.

MARCUS. It was his account. He sued the production company. He was out on his ass before he knew what hit him. And six months go by, and nobody answers his calls, and it's not like he's some kid and it's no big deal. He's a middle-aged man and it's a very big deal. So what's he do? What's he do? What's he do? He drives his fuckin' Volvo off the Palisades Cliffs!

ANDREA. He was a good man.

MARCUS. Gave me a lotta work.

ANDREA. Plenty of people aren't worried. They just want to shoot in Miami in February, and if the spot sells the cereal, you know, or whatever, then everybody's happy.

MARCUS. But what if it doesn't — if it doesn't sell the cereal?

ANDREA. Carl Havens.

MARCUS. Fear is our friend, boys. You're home. You're watching your idiot box. You see some creamy pink crap. It looks good. You want to buy it. That's all that matters. Go ahead and take the client to Miami. Feed him at Joe's Stone Crabs. But you better remember the pink crap, 'cause it's a commercial about pink crap.

ANDREA. It's the hero.

MARCUS. Jeffrey, what's a prop man call a fifteen-hundred-dollar, color-corrected, camera-ready cup full of sugar water?

JEFFREY. A hero.

MARCUS. A hero. And he should. 'Cause that's where the money is.

ANDREA. *(Checking her watch.)* So ...

MARCUS. There should be a museum: a Museum of American Advertising Art.

ANDREA. We've got —

MARCUS. That's right. I said ART. The Broadcast Museum: That's just a lotta noise. I know about cultural theory. Art has to stop time. And no TV show can stop time 'cause TV shows need to *take* time to lead you to — what? Anyone? —

RON. Commercials.

MARCUS. Commercials! The shows are all set up to suck you in, and sit you down so you see some commercials. The shows are a lie. The commercials are the truth. They're the only thing that's complete, that's not interrupted. People all say that they hate the commercials. Why do they say that? 'Cause they *love* the commercials! Commercials are meat; the shows are just a lotta mayonnaise. *(The intercom beeps and Andrea punches a button on the phone as she picks up the receiver.)*

ANDREA. Yeah. *(Andrea holds out the receiver for Marcus.)* Jerry Golding on five.

MARCUS. What's he want? More freebies? Fuckin' guy's gonna bankrupt me. *(Marcus snatches the receiver from Andrea, punches*

33

line five on the phone, and suddenly sounds warm and compassionate.) Jerry … *(Beat.)* Who cares about me, how you doin'? How's Sammy? How's that fever? *(Beat.)* Hey, thank goodness. I mean, thank goodness. The chicken pox isn't just the chicken pox, Jerry. The chicken pox is the chicken pox. I remember the chicken pox — nobody called. But if anybody had or anybody does, I'll take care of you, babe. Let me be the bad guy … *(Beat.)* No, I know that. I want to. I'm happy to. All that matters is we bring you your shots and, I'm telling you, Jerry, you're gonna have 'em. In spades. Look, Jerry … Jerry … Hey, come on now, it's me here, buddy. Tomorrow you're gonna sit there in front of these dailies and smile like a hero. Like a conquering hero. *(Beat.)* Okay, now, sweetheart. This is for you. It's all for you. Okay? Okay, now. Buh-bye. *(Marcus hangs up and turns on Andrea.)* That cheap prick.

ANDREA. I know.

MARCUS. He spends a few bucks in post and we don't even have to be here today.

ANDREA. Maybe.

MARCUS. You saw the dailies. They're not that far off. *(A quick look from Andrea.)* Okay, they're off, okay? But they could fix it. It's just easier to come crying to me. Fucking Jerry fucking GOLDING.

ANDREA. Golding's got a lot of work coming up and you know it.

MARCUS. I don't have to like it.

ANDREA. Did he talk about the timing on the turntable?

MARCUS. Oh, for Chrissake —

ANDREA. Marcus. He just wants you to check it. So we're sure.

MARCUS. So he's got someone else he can blame.

ANDREA. Golding's got three weeks of Breyers Ice Cream in December and you're recommended on that —

MARCUS. I better be.

ANDREA. They're gonna bid it in Chicago.

MARCUS. They are not —

ANDREA. It's a big job, Marcus. Six hundred grand. For ice cream, which you can shoot in your sleep. Now you wanna bend, or you wanna bend over?

MARCUS. Have I mentioned how much I like Jerry Golding?

ANDREA. That's what I wanna hear. *(Marcus glances at Jeffrey and Ron.)*

MARCUS. Get 'em nervous. *(Marcus heads off and Andrea crosses to the set.)*
ANDREA. Can I heat 'em up?
JEFFREY. We're close.
ANDREA. How close? We've gotta go. Tense up guys.
JEFFREY. I've still got work to do.
ANDREA. You're killing me. He's killing me. Five minutes. I mean it. FIVE MINUTES! *(Andrea storms off.)*
DAVE. How does the Director's Guild test them, anyway: How do they know she's a real bitch and not just pretending?
OSCAR. I don't know, but it's foolproof — not a lot o' sweet ones slippin' through.
JEFFREY. *(Rummaging through an equipment box.)* Shit.
RON. What are you looking for?
JEFFREY. Duvateen. Duvateen. Where is the goddamn duvateen?
RON. It's where it always is. *(Jeffrey slams the lid of the equipment box.)*
JEFFREY. Gimme a scrap.
RON. What's the matter?
JEFFREY. I'm not gonna make it.
RON. Sure you are.
JEFFREY. The whole thing's overworked. I can't even see what I'm doing. Too much tinkering —
RON. Take 'em one at a time.
JEFFREY. They're slumping under.
RON. You need a better armature.
JEFFREY. What?
RON. Try a ball of blackwrap. *(Ron pulls a roll of black aluminum foil from the equipment box and tears off a small piece.)*
JEFFREY. Anything. I don't care.
RON. You can shape it. It's gonna be good.
JEFFREY. God, my hands are shaking.
RON. That's Marcus. The mind of Marcus. Making us miserable. It's such a shame. This stuff should really be fun. But you have to care. I guess that's the trick. He needs to see you care. *(Ron hands Jeffrey the molded piece of foil.)*
JEFFREY. What is this?
RON. Put it in the middle — just to lift it out.

JEFFREY. Whatever. *(Ron picks up a length of wire and cuts it with his pocket pliers.)*
RON. We do care. We do, don't we, Jeffrey? Because we're artisans. In the thirteenth century we'd be carving the gargoyles on a Gothic cathedral. But now we build our tallest towers for trade, not devotion, which means that money is the new God. And we all pray for money. But we also have these improbable opportunities to actually work with our hands. *(Handing Jeffrey the piece of wire.)* Put in a piece of floral wire.
JEFFREY. Where?
RON. Wrap it around the stem.
JEFFREY. *(Taking the wire.)* I am learning to hate these grapes. *(Ron places a pushpin into a wooden plinth.)*
RON. Put a pushpin behind the cup and use it as a pick point.
JEFFREY. Hey. That's good. I like that.
RON. Same over here.
JEFFREY. Wait a second. It's easy. I can brace it from behind.
RON. That's the idea.
JEFFREY. It's actually a better way.
RON. I think so.
JEFFREY. Gimme another piece. *(Jeffrey snatches another piece of wire from Ron.)*
RON. So, what I was saying is: We could consider ourselves part of an ancient artistic tradition. We don't make valuable stuff anymore, but at least we make memorable images. And the images themselves have a certain human energy.
JEFFREY. Ron, I hate to burst your bubble here, but we're not artisans. We're technicians. And there's a big difference.
RON. Technically, I guess.
JEFFREY. Look at your time card. It says "LABOR." It doesn't say, you know, "FUN." We're not even supposed to know what we're doing. We're supposed to just do it, okay? We implement. We do not invent. We're limbs, okay? Arms and fingers, not hearts and minds.
RON. I know. I'm just saying. What if we were?
JEFFREY. What if we were what?
RON. Inventors. Renaissance men. There's something so pure about what we're doing. We're like these divine wing-footed mes-

sengers who carry the answers to every human need. And the messages that we, the true creators of advertising, are entrusted to deliver, these messages of ours, they actually improve the world. They do. They definitely do. I mean, think about it. What are we saying today? "Enjoy your life! Have more fun! Drink a frozen fruit concoction!"

JEFFREY. You are such a putz.

RON. Oh, am I?

JEFFREY. In every way. We're not messengers, Ron, we're snake oil salesmen. We are creating needs, not satisfying them. We're helping Americans grow increasingly obese, bringing them new sorts of artificial sweeteners, new kinds of carcinogens, new pieces of unnecessary plastic. If something is actually good for you, Ron, it doesn't get a television commercial. When was the last time you saw a spot for organic asparagus? But we'll happily dedicate billions of dollars and hours to snack cakes and fizzy beverages. We corrupt the children, depress the adults and destroy the last dregs of independent thinking. That is our profession, Ron. That is what they're paying us for.

RON. So you think we'd all be better off if we, you know, if we just hunkered down along a riverbank and ate crayfish and dandelion greens?

JEFFREY. I think so.

RON. Sorry, Jeffrey, but I happen to like what we do.

JEFFREY. 'Cause you don't know what we do.

OSCAR. You boys wanna take this outside?

JEFFREY. Dolly in, Oscar. Dave, open the eyepiece. I'm gonna need a work light.

OSCAR. Watch your eyes. *(Oscar throws the bull switch and adjusts a dimmer, bringing the set lights to a soft glow.)*

JEFFREY. What's the word?

DAVE. You're almost there.

JEFFREY. Let me look. *(Jeffrey moves to the monitor.)*

RON. Talk to me.

JEFFREY. On the camera left orange.

RON. On the orange.

JEFFREY. Slide it slowly camera right.

RON. Going right.

JEFFREY. Stop. Back a bit. Hold that. Good. The grapes are good.

OSCAR. Real good. Right on. Look at that.

DAVE. Nice.

RON. Thanks.

JEFFREY. What's that spot?

RON. Sorry?

JEFFREY. On the apple.

RON. Where?

JEFFREY. At the top.

RON. Here?

JEFFREY. What is it?

RON. *(Quietly.)* It's that bruise.

JEFFREY. That's what I was afraid of.

RON. *(Turning the apple.)* If we clock it ever so slightly on axis —

JEFFREY. It won't match.

RON. It'd be better.

JEFFREY. Take it counter.

RON. I could maybe tilt it —

JEFFREY. Just lock it, Ron. Leave it. Walk away.

RON. Walking away.

JEFFREY. Save the lights. *(Oscar shuts off the bull switch.)*

RON. Good job, Jeffrey. Really. It looks great. *(Ron hands Jeffrey a spray bottle. They continue working. Dave tries to take Oscar aside.)*

DAVE. I'm sorry about the store.

OSCAR. Forget it, man.

DAVE. I wanted to do it — I honestly did.

OSCAR. You never told me the girl's name.

JEFFREY. Girl?

OSCAR. Davie's got some new sugar.

JEFFREY. Does he, then?

OSCAR. Mmm-hmm.

DAVE. I don't want to make a big deal of it, Oscar.

JEFFREY. Too late now. Sorry. Is she cute?

DAVE. I happen to think so.

OSCAR. Nice tits?

DAVE. I can't complain.

JEFFREY. Oranges? Grapefruits? Vine-ripened honeydews?

DAVE. Portabella mushrooms, actually. *(They all take a moment*

to think about this.)
OSCAR. With the fuzzy side down?
DAVE. Right.
OSCAR. Sorta like Andrea's?
DAVE. Somewhat.
OSCAR. I like 'em like that.
RON. Anyway, uh, what I was gonna say is, I've been giving this whole thing some thought, and I'm pretty sure there's this whole other way we could do tabletop, you know, where we don't just try for what one guy wants, but we all get together and find what works.
OSCAR. No, Ron.
JEFFREY. Never.
OSCAR. You're a soldier, son. You stay in step. You start to wonder where you wanna march, you gonna be bangin' around like a goddamn clown.
RON. This isn't the army, Oscar, this is actually considered a creative profession.
JEFFREY. Not for you.
RON. There are such things as artists, Jeffrey.
JEFFREY. Artists are food. Okay? They come in here and fag around for a few minutes with their fabric swatches and flower arrangements and then they're chewed up and shat out. Artists are plankton; Marcus is the whale. *(Beat.)* Listen, Ron, you want to hear how it works?
RON. No. Actually. I don't think I do.
JEFFREY. *(As he practices his pour.)* This liquid, this luscious stream of liquid, is what it's all about. And there's this corporation with these stockholders and this board of directors. And they're gonna start making a lot of money off this liquid. And sales will create jobs. And jobs will create sales. And this liquid is like *blood* and we're here at the *aorta* of capitalism, okay? And all that blood is rushing right by. And it's rich. And it's oxygenated. And we can't spill a drop. If we can manage to not spill a drop, we get to stick around and drink, don't we? But only if we don't fuck up. That's all that really matters. Not fucking up.
RON. You don't really believe that.
JEFFREY. It's the truth.
RON. You're saying it's the safest guy — not the smartest, not the

more inventive or the more inspired — no, no, the safest, the stupidest, the stubbornest. Is that how cynical you are?

JEFFREY. That's right.

RON. It's the scum, not the cream, that rises to the top?

JEFFREY. It's a complicated issue, Ron.

RON. Oh, so it's not a matter of scum versus cream. We're really talking about creamy scum. Or scummy cream. Some sort of contaminated cappuccino ...

JEFFREY. Sorry, you lost me there.

DAVE. You have to want it more than anyone else.

RON, JEFFREY and OSCAR. What?

JEFFREY. Quiet man speaks.

OSCAR. Dave, don't feel you have to participate.

DAVE. This is primitive. The causes aren't entirely clear. It could be genetics or infant trauma or sibling rivalry, but Marcus wants this work more than anything any one of us can even imagine. Actually, it's greater than want. It's need. The rest of us, you know, we might like to run the show, sure. We have our little fantasies. But for Marcus, this is air. He needs it to breathe. And he'll push us down, shove our heads under water, whatever it takes to keep breathing.

RON. God, that's depressing.

OSCAR. Why don't you give us the real dirt, Dave?

DAVE. Oscar ...

OSCAR. Come on, man, talk about the skirt. Does she butter your carrot? He ain't askin' for much, he just lookin' for some touch!

JEFFREY. What kind of touch are we talkin' about?

RON. Guys —

JEFFREY. Is there any hand lotion involved?

RON. You are such a perv.

OSCAR. You ever seen a Brazilian bikini wax?

DAVE. Um, no, Oscar.

OSCAR. That's some kinda sushi dinner.

DAVE. Oscar, I don't want to play this.

OSCAR. Why not? If we can't talk about pussy, we can't talk at all.

DAVE. You can still have the store, Oscar.

OSCAR. Pussy, Dave, pussy.

JEFFREY. "The password is … pussy."

DAVE. Okay. Okay. So, what we do … what we do is we make everything take the longest possible time. Like, last night (and I am not exaggerating) I must have spent well over an hour just unbuttoning this shirt.

JEFFREY. Are you high?

DAVE. I think I am a little, yes, or at least I was, as I was tracing that tendon at the neck and tasting a tiny freckle at the triangle above the collarbone, and inhaling this rain-forest fragrance of hair, the sweet swelling of the chest, and then lingering, going, slowly, down, button to button, taking each disc of milky plastic between my fingertips, slipping it from a sewn slit in soft cotton, one by one, opening, releasing, scent and sinew, revealing the smooth wonder of a firm white belly, the bow of a back, that vertebral curve, that arch that ends at a pelvis pushing forward, entreating, pleading to at least be touched, rippling and rising and tempting me, but I take my time — the body begs me but I take my time — because I want, and I want all the wanting, the sighing, the straining to somehow stay, to stop (and to not even breathe), to loll in the liquid deliciousness of desire. *(Silence.)*

RON. Whoa.

JEFFREY. Dave.

OSCAR. Lord have mercy.

JEFFREY. *(Covering his crotch with a plastic pitcher.)* Guy's givin' me a woody.

OSCAR. Red alert.

RON. Stand clear.

JEFFREY. Code one. *(Dave crosses to camera, looking busy for effect. Oscar sets a stand. Andrea and Marcus march in.)*

DAVE. Okay, dolly's on its marks?

OSCAR. Right where we were.

MARCUS. Can we do this now?

JEFFREY. Props are ready.

ANDREA. House lights out.

OSCAR. Watch your eyes. *(Oscar slams the bull switch.)*

MARCUS. What do we have on the key?

DAVE. That's an eight-eleven.

MARCUS. Check it again on the edge of the cup.

41

DAVE. Eight-eleven, sir.

MARCUS. You trimmed the key light?

OSCAR. Cutter on the ten-K.

MARCUS. Good. Okay. Looks good. Move the fill a little closer.

OSCAR. On the fill.

MARCUS. Back it off. Good. Hold that. *(Studying his setup through the eyepiece.)* This looks good. I like it. It looks fuller than before.

RON. *(Unconsciously.)* Thanks.

ANDREA. What did you do to the grapes, Jeffrey?

JEFFREY. I've got them wired from behind.

MARCUS. Smart.

ANDREA. How's the liquid?

MARCUS. Looks thin.

JEFFREY. I better start from scratch. *(Jeffrey dumps his tired liquid into a slop bucket, then removes a fresh pouch from the cooler and pours it into his bowl. During the following, he beats the mixture with a wire whisk, occasionally checking its consistency.)*

ANDREA. He's gonna need another minute.

MARCUS. Take your time, Jeffrey.

ANDREA. Cool the lights.

OSCAR. *(Shutting off the bull switch.)* Cooling.

MARCUS. Get it right.

JEFFREY. I'm sorry. You want it to have that thickness.

MARCUS. It's worth the wait. Watch and learn, boys. The hands of a master. *(Beat.)* Oscar, I hear you need help with your store.

OSCAR. Well, I might.

MARCUS. You just say the word.

OSCAR. Thank you, sir.

MARCUS. What happened to *you*, Dave?

ANDREA. Not now, Marcus.

MARCUS. I'm just asking.

JEFFREY. *(Changing the subject.)* So, you gonna hit the yard sales this weekend?

MARCUS. Yeah. Probably. Sunday.

OSCAR. You've got it all sussed, don't you?

JEFFREY. You've got a whole system. You get up early. You check the local paper. What's it called — *The Penny Saver*?

MARCUS. Some such shit. It's easy. It's like shooting fish in a barrel. Especially the farmers. I hit them first. They never know what they have. The stuff I've stolen from these people, it's unbelievable. Like last Sunday, I'm at this dairy barn, right? And it's Ma and Pa with the pitchfork and the overalls. What's that? What do they call that?

OSCAR. *American Gothic?*

MARCUS. Right. And they've got the usual crap, you know, the flatware and old clothes and broken bicycles. And then I see this cherry side table. Musta been in the fucking farmhouse for two hundred years. It's fucking filthy. And it's a great piece. Pegged and dovetailed. Beautiful. And when they're not looking I wipe away some of the grime with my thumb and I see the color of this wood and I mean it's perfect. It's that perfect patina with the nicks and the burns and the old oil finish. Like if we ever do Kraft or Country Crock — any of that homey cozy crap.

JEFFREY. Like that shot last month with the grated cheese.

OSCAR. Taco Rico.

MARCUS. Exactly. That's exactly what I was thinking: Taco Rico. So I get 'em down to like a hundred and fifty bucks. It's fucking pathetic. And then Pa starts saying: "You can clean it up. You're really gonna love it. It's perfect for a nice young couple." I gave 'em some line of shit that it was a surprise for my wife.

ANDREA. You have no shame.

MARCUS. I never said I did. And so anyway, Ma and Pa, right? They follow me out to my car. You know, I try to shake 'em, but this is obviously their big sale of the day. They walk me all the way down to the road. And I have the Mercedes that day, okay? So Pa says, "Maybe I can find some rope and tie it to the roof of the car." And I just quietly open the trunk, and pull out my little Jap saw, and I start cutting the legs off the table with the two of them standing there.

OSCAR. Damn.

JEFFREY. I love it.

ANDREA. You're too cruel.

MARCUS. I didn't ask them to follow me. It was their fault. I'm using the piece for tabletop. I need a nice surface under the cheddar cheese. I'm just gonna throw it on sawhorses.

ANDREA. You could've let them tie it to your car.

MARCUS. And scratch the paint?

OSCAR. Can't have that.

JEFFREY. So what did you say?

MARCUS. Nothing. They just stood there and watched me like I was butchering their family dog. Their mouths were sort of half-open. It was hilarious. Then I said "thank you," which I didn't have to say, and I got in my car and drove away.

RON. Did you take the legs?

MARCUS. What?

RON. The table legs.

MARCUS. No. I just left 'em on the ground. What am I gonna do with some fucking table legs? *(Ron is mortified. Andrea looks to Jeffrey.)*

ANDREA. You ready?

JEFFREY. Standing by. *(Everyone but Ron heads back to camera.)*

ANDREA. Let's get set to go. Oscar, gimme a glow. Ron, just spritz the grapes and check the surface. Ron? *(Oscar throws the bull switch and then dims down the set lights to a soft amber glow.)*

JEFFREY. Yo. Ron. Hello.

MARCUS. Goddamn it, can we get someone in here who knows what he's doing? *(Ron snaps out of it and approaches the tabletop with a dust brush and spritzer.)*

RON. Flying in ... I just gotta cut through the underbrush. *(Ron pushes the front fill card out of his way.)*

ANDREA. Got a mark on that?

MARCUS. What's he doing?

ANDREA. He's gotta get in there.

MARCUS. He's gotta relight my set?

ANDREA. Ron ...

RON. I need to get to the fruit.

MARCUS. That stand was locked! It was a lock! What are you fuckin' doin'?

ANDREA. He's got it marked.

RON. Thank you.

MARCUS. He's got shit.

ANDREA. Come on, just check the frame. *(Marcus looks through the eyepiece.)*

MARCUS. Get that out of there.

RON. What?

MARCUS. By the banana.

RON. The raspberry?

MARCUS. Lose it.

RON. *(Reaching in with pocket pliers.)* Losing it.

MARCUS. What's with the apple?

RON. The apple?

MARCUS. What's that schmutz at the top?

RON. It's a discoloration.

MARCUS. Was it there before?

JEFFREY. I believe we had it angled another way.

MARCUS. So clock it; clock the raggedy-ass piece of fruit.

RON. Clocking.

MARCUS. Shit. *(Marcus crosses to Andrea at the video cart.)*

ANDREA. You want to swap it out? Go get another one, Jeffrey. I got six cases. *(Jeffrey glares at Ron, then slowly descends the ladder, circles down around the set just to buy time. As Marcus curses sotto voce to Andrea, Ron reaches into the fruit arrangement and makes a quick adjustment.)*

RON. How's that?

MARCUS. *(To Andrea.)* What'd he do?

ANDREA. He tilted it.

RON. It's like Cézanne.

MARCUS. What?

RON. This ... French ... guy.

MARCUS. I know Cézanne.

RON. This is just like his still lives, Marcus. I really think. I mean, I was just looking at what you've got and it's so beautiful. *(Marcus studies his composition on the monitor at the video cart. He sees what Ron means. And he begins to soften.)*

MARCUS. *(Pointing to a shape on the monitor.)* This distortion here ...

RON. Right! It bends and it pushes, but it finds a kind of balance. It's impossible but it's perfect.

MARCUS. *Fruit Bowl, Glass, and Apples.*

RON. *(Recalling the reference.)* Oh my God ...

JEFFREY. *(Irked.)* You gonna spritz the grapes?

RON. I'm on that. *(To Marcus, with a little French accent.)* And we like my little tilt on ze app-elle?

MARCUS. Andrea, get him outta there.

RON. So you're happy?

MARCUS. Andrea …

RON. Spritzing.

MARCUS. I SAID OUT!

ANDREA. Ron, just get up and get out. *(Ron stops what he's doing and starts trying to extract himself from the set as Marcus looks in the lens.)*

MARCUS. Oscar, gimme the fill.

RON. I got it.

MARCUS. I said Oscar.

RON. Okay. *(Oscar sets the card in its position.)*

MARCUS. Let's shoot this beast before I get any older.

ANDREA. Lights up. *(Oscar fades up the set lights on the dimmer.)*

MARCUS. You ready, Jeffrey?

JEFFREY. Standing by.

ANDREA. Are you ready on video?

OSCAR. Standing by.

MARCUS. Stop down.

DAVE. Stopping down.

ANDREA. Roll tape.

OSCAR. Tape speed.

ANDREA. Camera. *(The photosonics camera revs up.)*

DAVE. SPEED! *(Jeffrey uneventfully pours the liquid.)*

MARCUS. AND CUT!

ANDREA. Lights.

MARCUS. Nice. Gimme playback. *(Indicating the large downstage monitor.)* Put it up over here, Oscar.

OSCAR. Playback.

DAVE. Camera reloads.

ANDREA. Make it quick. Oscar, cue it up. Ron, Jeffrey, reset.

OSCAR. Three hundred and sixty frames.

JEFFREY. That's how it's done, my friend. It's simple. It's simple. It's so fucking simple.

ANDREA. Check the counter.

OSCAR. Three hundred sixty. *(Marcus watches as a perfect pour appears.)*

MARCUS. Hey, now. Look at that. You see that thickness there?

(Jeffrey joins Marcus at the monitor.)
JEFFREY. Got that twist.
MARCUS. Oh, that's pretty.
ANDREA. Nice.
JEFFREY. "The nape of a neck."
MARCUS. That's the shape. Oh yeah. You see that curve? You see the muscle there? I like that. There. Look. Wooo. That is what I like. That is what I wanted. Golding's gonna die! *(Playback continues and shows the liquid slopping over the side of the cup, splattering the fruit. The take we're all watching is Ron's.)*
MARCUS. What is this?
OSCAR. I cued the wrong take.
ANDREA. *(Over to Oscar.)* Watch your numbers. *(Now to Marcus.)* You want to move on? *(Marcus doesn't answer.)* We've got this. That was perfect. We only need two seconds. We'll cut away before the spill. Marcus, we've still gotta get to the swirl. We should at least start setting it up. *(Tension.)*
RON. You're not gonna say anything?
MARCUS. What?
RON. About my pour?
MARCUS. What? What about it? You just wasted my time.
RON. It wasn't wasted.
MARCUS. What?
RON. I didn't waste it, Marcus, you just stood there and said —
MARCUS. You got lucky. You went off and you pissed in the wind and now you wanna call it a special effect. Whadda you know? I'll tell you who knows: Jeffrey knows. 'Cause Jeffrey does his job —
ANDREA. Okay, Marcus.
MARCUS. Listen. Listen to me. I am tired of your mouth. I don't wanna hear another peep out of you. I'm serious. I'm dead serious. I don't even wanna know you're here!
ANDREA. So, are we moving on?
MARCUS. Do one more for luck.
ANDREA. We've got Jeffrey's for luck.
MARCUS. Inexcusable — fuckin' inexcusable. *(Marcus exits.)*
ANDREA. All right. Set it up. We're going again. Two minutes, Jeffrey.

JEFFREY. Two minutes. *(Andrea follows Marcus and exits.)*

RON. Did his parents beat him or just starve him?

OSCAR. Just lay low.

RON. Maybe they had, like, a stun gun or a cattle prod or something.

JEFFREY. Take it easy.

RON. I know. It's weird. When he treats you like an idiot, you sort of become an idiot somehow.

OSCAR. We've all been there, man.

RON. He can shred anyone at any time, can't he? Oscar, if there's a flare down the barrel. Dave, if the focus is off. Andrea, if she leaves the shot list in the bathroom. Jeffrey … No, not Jeffrey. Jeff's his little favorite son. *(Andrea enters.)*

ANDREA. So is anyone planning to show me this swirl?

JEFFREY. Sure.

RON. *(Crossing.)* No.

ANDREA. What's the problem?

JEFFREY. I got it right here.

RON. *(To Jeffrey.)* It's been sitting around too long. It's probably gone all lacy. Let me make a fresh one. *(Ron grabs the little Igloo cooler and heads offstage as Marcus enters.)*

DAVE. Battle stations. *(Everyone gets busy.)*

OSCAR. Watch your eyes. *(Oscar throws the bull switch. The intercom beeps.)*

MARCUS. Let's bang one out. *(Andrea picks up the receiver, listens, then …)*

ANDREA. Golding.

MARCUS. Awww —

ANDREA. He wants to talk about the timing.

MARCUS. Let Stevie grease him. Tell some stories. Talk about the golf courses in Scotland.

ANDREA. He needs an answer now.

MARCUS. I'm under enough pressure already.

ANDREA. So is he.

MARCUS. Fine, fine, fine. Let's do it. What's the copy?

ANDREA. *(To Oscar.)* Cool the lights. *(To the receptionist.)* We'll call back in five. *(Andrea hangs up the phone. Oscar hits the bull switch. Andrea crosses to Marcus and shows him her clipboard.)* Right

here. This is it. "The New Fruit Freeze from Chicken Lickin'."
That's a no-brainer. That's just basic: You hear the voice-over, you
pick up the slow-motion pour.
MARCUS. Uh-huh.
ANDREA. Jerry's just gotta tell them about frame twenty-three.
(Holding her stopwatch.) "Cup rotates to reveal logo over closing
voice-over."
MARCUS. Right.
ANDREA. *(Quickly.)* Thing is, Jerry's question is: Do we reveal
the logo on "value" or do we pick up on the move and reveal it
halfway through the line?
MARCUS. What?
ANDREA. *(Clicking the stopwatch.)* "Welcome to our world of
value." *(Clicking the stopwatch again.)* I get like two-point-one sec-
onds on the line, right?
MARCUS. *(Not really understanding.)* Okay.
ANDREA. The shot's boarded for two-point-five, so when do we
reveal the logo?
MARCUS. What's Jerry think?
ANDREA. He wants to know what you think.
MARCUS. That prick.
ANDREA. Just tell him what you think.
MARCUS. It's his commercial.
ANDREA. *(Clicking the stopwatch.)* "Welcome to our world of
value." *(Click.)* Two and change. *(Clicking.)* "Welcome to our
worrrld of valllue." *(Click.)* Two-point-five exactly. Somebody's
gotta make up his mind.
MARCUS. He has extra frames on the head and tail. He can do
a dissolve or something. What's his fucking problem?
ANDREA. He's your client. He wants a straight answer.
MARCUS. Get 'em out.
ANDREA. What?
MARCUS. Out. Out. Everyone out!
ANDREA. What's the matter?
MARCUS. You. Me. My office. Now. *(Marcus exits. Shuts the
door. Silence.)*
JEFFREY. Somebody needs a diaper change.
ANDREA. Where's Ron?

JEFFREY. Why?

ANDREA. What do you mean, "Why?"

JEFFREY. He's in the prop room.

ANDREA. Listen, I need you guys to hang by Hector at the loading dock. Get those boxes off the ramp. Put all the practical product in storage. And have someone stay by the intercom.

JEFFREY. I'll get Ron.

OSCAR. *(Blocking Jeffrey's way.)* Leave him alone.

JEFFREY. That's a bad idea.

OSCAR. MOVE! *(The guys file out. Andrea exits to the office. Dave furtively returns, picks up the phone and dials.)*

DAVE. *(Into the phone.)* Yes, this is David Hayes. May I speak with James Herrington please. Thank you. *(Beat.)* Hi. No. I'm on set. Um, no, I don't. I mean, I can't. But I did want to tell you: I told them. Yeah, I did. I left it sort of deliberately vague. Don't worry. We'll be fine. *(Ron peeks in, holding the little Igloo cooler. He sees Dave. Dave sees him.)*

RON. Hi.

DAVE. *(Into the phone.)* I can't talk right now. I just wanted you to know that I will be there. I'll be there. *(Beat.)* YOU are my priority. I want to do this. This is what I want. Likewise. Yes, that's what I said. That's all I can say. *(Dave hangs up the phone.)*

RON. I didn't mean to sneak up on you.

DAVE. It's okay.

RON. Where is everybody?

DAVE. The loading dock.

RON. Whoa, that place is way too gross for me. Everyone just standing there shivering and smoking cigarettes. And there's always like a used condom in the crack by the fire door and a frozen glob of spit on the cement and then Jeffrey lets like a big, sulphurous fart and blames it on me.

DAVE. Ron.

RON. Yeah.

DAVE. You really do think about things more than you ought to.

RON. I know.

DAVE. Try to work on it.

RON. I will. Sorry. Was that Jim?

DAVE. James.

RON. He's your lover, isn't he?

DAVE. Please don't use that word. You call a man a lover and you set off this instant little montage of pornographic videos in people's heads. Really, it's tacky.

RON. What word do you use?

DAVE. Nothing — "Boyfriend." "Roommate." "Beau."

RON. Beau?

DAVE. It means handsome.

RON. Yeah, I know, I've been to France.

DAVE. Look, I'm sure it seems a bit quaint of me, Ron, but I'm not comfortable talking about this here, not even with you.

RON. I understand.

DAVE. No you don't.

RON. Dave, I don't mean to —

DAVE. Yes you do. *(Andrea enters and Dave quietly exits.)*

ANDREA. Is that the new hero?

RON. This is it. *(Ron reveals the swirl and Andrea swoons.)*

ANDREA. Incredible.

RON. Think it'll fly?

ANDREA. It's creamy. It's so creamy. How did he make it so creamy?

RON. Who?

ANDREA. Jeffrey. *(Ron turns away.)* It wasn't Jeffrey, was it?

RON. It was me. Oops. I wasn't supposed to say anything, but you asked.

ANDREA. Okay, listen. Leave this here with me. I want you to go back in the shop and work out a turntable.

RON. *(Unsure.)* Sure.

ANDREA. Make it steady. Solid. A Mack truck.

RON. Actually ...

ANDREA. Lock it all off within an inch of its life.

RON. I had this other idea —

ANDREA. No, Ron. Nothing fancy. Safe. Play it safe.

RON. I didn't say fancy.

ANDREA. Just give him his turntable. Your swirl. And his turntable.

RON. Okay, but —

ANDREA. No buts.

RON. Okay.

ANDREA. Okay. *(Ron exits. Andrea takes a moment to adore the swirl, then collapses onto the sofa. Dave enters, tiptoes to the phone, begins to dial, and then senses Andrea watching him.)*

ANDREA. It can't be easy, can it?

DAVE. What?

ANDREA. Anything. Ever.

DAVE. I was on my way out.

ANDREA. Dave.

DAVE. I'll be downstairs.

ANDREA. Can we just discuss this for a second.

DAVE. Don't even try.

ANDREA. He's extremely unhappy.

DAVE. So am I.

ANDREA. What is it? A family thing? Someone coming for the weekend?

DAVE. Andrea. I'm not available and that's all I need to tell you.

ANDREA. He asked me what you're doing, Dave.

DAVE. It's social, okay?

ANDREA. Oh, Dave, please.

DAVE. A very close friend is being honored by a major professional organization in his field and it's a big deal for this person which makes it a big deal for me and so I promised I'd be there and I'm keeping that promise.

ANDREA. What person?

DAVE. This guy — he's like my best friend.

ANDREA. So send him a card.

DAVE. You're not hearing me, Andrea.

ANDREA. It's just a little hard to explain, Dave. If you'll forgive me, Marcus gives you how many days a year? — plus plenty of time-and-a-half and double-time. It's fair to say that you owe the man a little consideration.

DAVE. What does he owe me?

ANDREA. Not a lot.

DAVE. Please, Andrea, help me out.

ANDREA. I'll try to think of something I can say. *(Marcus storms in and Dave exits.)*

MARCUS. I swear to God, if he tells me one more time about his fifty-three hundred shipments and his walk-in refrigerators and his franchise managers —

ANDREA. You're gonna make it, Marcus.

MARCUS. A six A.M. transfer at Du Art? No, Andrea, I don't think so. I'm not gonna knock off this shot in an hour. *(Andrea holds up the hero cup.)* Oh ... my ... God.

ANDREA. Care to revise your opinion?

MARCUS. God in heaven. That is exactly what Jerry was talking about.

ANDREA. I know.

MARCUS. We can shoot the sucker just like it is.

ANDREA. I know.

MARCUS. Who did this?

ANDREA. I take care of you, Marcus, that's all I do. I can even ask Golding for an overage. He'd give it to you.

MARCUS. I got a better idea.

ANDREA. Ice cream.

MARCUS. Exactly. We'll get it. We've got to.

ANDREA. We will.

MARCUS. You think we can nail down Sizzler?

ANDREA. Don't get greedy.

MARCUS. What?

ANDREA. You don't have time for a conference call.

MARCUS. The hell I don't.

ANDREA. You've got a crew standing around downstairs.

MARCUS. So get 'em up. Rough something in. Have 'em rehearse.

ANDREA. I heard from Bill Davis.

MARCUS. Yeah?

ANDREA. His pizza thing went away.

MARCUS. Went away where?

ANDREA. We're dead all next month.

MARCUS. We've got Spaghetti-O's. We'll get Stove Top.

ANDREA. Trash for cash.

MARCUS. We'll get Breyers.

ANDREA. Listen —

MARCUS. They give us our mark-up.

ANDREA. That's not what you need.

MARCUS. What do I need?

ANDREA. A real job, Marcus. A commercial, not an insert. A major campaign. Something you'll wanna show on the street.
MARCUS. Who said this?
ANDREA. You know it. You said it. Just look at your reel.
MARCUS. I like my reel.
ANDREA. It's too mid-nineties.
MARCUS. For Chrissake, Andrea, I'm not gonna fingerpaint like these kid creatives. I'm not gonna put a ring in my eyelid. I'm not gonna bang a goddamn hard light into a hamburger!
ANDREA. Hold on. Hear me out. All those shots from Chicago —
MARCUS. God help us.
ANDREA. If you had to say one thing you like about them —
MARCUS. Please.
ANDREA. There's a kind of wit, though, isn't there? They're fun. The guy's stuff is fun, Marcus. It's so free and loose and off-the-cuff. You could work like that; it wouldn't kill you. You know what it reminds me of? Your studio manager.
MARCUS. Are you insane?
ANDREA. You need Ron. You don't even know, Marcus. He's the thing. He's what they all want. He's what's selling.
MARCUS. He's a fuckup.
ANDREA. Everyone fucks up.
MARCUS. He fucks up more.
ANDREA. He's like a battered child.
MARCUS. Oh yeah, that's nice, Andrea.
ANDREA. What I'm saying, is, Marcus, of course he fucks up —
MARCUS. He fucks ME up, okay? He's such a wuss. He makes me sick. He makes me physically sick.
ANDREA. He did this cup. You like this cup.
MARCUS. It's a fucking cup!
ANDREA. Okay, you win. *(Marcus exits. Andrea crosses to the craft service table, sifts through the array of food and selects a cookie, lifts it to her lips and takes a bite. Ron comes around the corner, carrying a mechanical rig. He put the rig down and watches Andrea.)*
RON. What are you doing here?
ANDREA. Chocolate.
RON. No, I mean … *(Ron sings to the Tom Jones tune.)* "What's a nice girl like you … doin' in a place like this?" Aren't you, like,

over it already? He treats you like a maid.

ANDREA. Ron, I billed two hundred and thirty-two days last year.

RON. Wow.

ANDREA. I'm fine.

RON. I guess so. You like that sixty-thousand-dollar sport utility vehicle ...

ANDREA. As a matter of fact, I do. I like my heated leather seats and my six-speaker stereo. I like sitting up above all the sedans and station wagons. I like that, Ron. I do. *(Andrea picks up the phone and punches a couple of buttons.)*

ANDREA. *(Into the receiver.)* Everybody up; we're moving on.

RON. You used to be married, didn't you?

ANDREA. Yup.

RON. To a gaffer?

ANDREA. That's right.

RON. Didn't want kids?

ANDREA. That's none of your business.

RON. No. It's your business. You just don't seem real happy to me. Neither does Marcus. I think that's why he hates me. Because I'm happy. This is just a theory. Anyway, my response is, "Okay, I'll just be a good boy and solve all his problems, and, eventually, you know, he'll notice." *(Marcus enters, head down, perusing a bid form.)*

MARCUS. Golding sent you some numbers on Breyers. *(Marcus sees Ron.)* What's he doing?

ANDREA. He's working. He's been working. Haven't you, Ron?

RON. Oh, most definitely. *(Marcus gives him a long look and then leaves.)*

ANDREA. Listen, you might want to keep a low profile this afternoon.

RON. Yeah, well, that's a little tough for me. As you may have noticed, I don't have a lot of protective coloration. Predators can sort of see me and eat me in one quick bite.

ANDREA. I showed him your swirl.

RON. He thinks it's Jeffrey —

ANDREA. No. I told him. Ron, Marcus needs your work. If he doesn't give Golding the prettiest little best-lit bit of frozen fruit drama, the next job he gets is gonna be a President's Day package for the tristate appliance dealers. He could drop right off the "A" list. You understand?

RON. Sort of.

ANDREA. Try to understand. Look, just gimme a solid lock-off. A nice motor, no twitch in the system.

RON. Okay.

ANDREA. And make me another hero.

RON. You got it. I'll do it. It'll be breathtaking. *(Andrea exits as Jeffrey, Oscar and Dave enter.)*

JEFFREY. Okay, Ron. Here's what we've got so far. She's medium height. Short dark hair. No tits whatsoever. She works part-time as a Panavision rep at the trade shows and she's shot some student films, but what she really loves to do is write poetry and read it out loud at — what's it called? — the "National Arts Club."

RON. On Gramercy Park.

JEFFREY. Whatever.

RON. I go to those readings.

OSCAR. Get outta town.

JEFFREY. I thought Dave was the gay boy.

RON. Seriously. Every Friday afternoon if we're not shooting. I've probably seen your beau — belle. *(A painful moment.)*

JEFFREY. Well, we are gathering vital information here.

RON. Is this an inquisition, Jeffrey?

DAVE. Seems to be. *(Ron carries his rig downstage.)*

RON. Hey. Check this out. What do you think?

JEFFREY. What the fuck?

RON. You remember on Friday they were all talking about making the move more dynamic — with maybe a tilt on the head or something — but then they thought it was too hard to coordinate? Okay, so, I put in this vertical axis under here, and it's like you get the rotation that they have in the board, but you can also combine it with this sort of heroic lift. Like Hamlet with Yorick's skull.

DAVE. You are incredible.

JEFFREY. Think it might be overkill? Ron, you can't just make what you want — this isn't arts and crafts, buddy.

RON. It's a solution.

JEFFREY. It's not what he wants.

RON. It's way better than what he wants.

JEFFREY. Where's the turntable?

RON. Right up top. See. Here. *(Andrea enters, eyes down on her clipboard.)*

ANDREA. How we doing?

RON. Fine and how are you?

ANDREA. Jeffrey, lock a stand-in on the turntable.

JEFFREY. I'd love to, but, as it turns out, Ron thinks he's found a better way —

DAVE. Shut up, Jeffrey.

ANDREA. Put up the twenty-eight to eighty-five. Find your marks. You know the lighting.

RON. Is someone gonna frame up the shot?

ANDREA. Do the best you can. Marcus is gonna get off this call and wanna grab one more take on the photosonics and move over here in a big rush —

JEFFREY. You don't want us caught with our pants around our ankles?

ANDREA. Exactly. Find a shot. Just get started. *(Andrea notices Ron's rig.)* Ron, what's this?

JEFFREY. Good question.

RON. It's the rig.

ANDREA. I didn't ask for a "rig." I asked for a turntable. A cup on a turntable.

JEFFREY. I told you.

ANDREA. What's this thing?

RON. An extra axis.

ANDREA. Jeffrey?

JEFFREY. Let me deal with it

ANDREA. I swear to God, Ron …

RON. This will work. I know what the guy is looking for. I heard the whole thing.

ANDREA. *(To Jeffrey.)* Get me the turntable just in case —

JEFFREY. Got it.

RON. You'll never need it. *(Andrea flips through her clipboard.)*

DAVE. Did you talk to Marcus?

ANDREA. Not yet, Dave.

OSCAR. Andrea, I've been thinking … I've made up my mind.

ANDREA. Oscar, this is a bad time —

OSCAR. You tell Marcus I'm taking that offer.

ANDREA. Terrific. He'll be pleased. It'll be good for both of us.

OSCAR. Tell him I appreciate it.

ANDREA. Oh, we know that, Oscar.

OSCAR. *(To Dave.)* You got that letter of agreement?

DAVE. Listen, Oscar, I know it's not my place, but I'm just not sure you've really had a chance to, you know, to consider the implications ...

OSCAR. You want me to listen to you?

DAVE. It's not about that —

OSCAR. Just give me the letter.

ANDREA. *(Overlapping.)* Look, I want everyone on this setup right away: That's the priority.

DAVE. *(To Oscar.)* Sure. I got it. It's right here. *(Dave pulls out the paper. He hands it to Oscar. Oscar passes it to Andrea.)*

ANDREA. You can rehearse —

RON. Rehearse what? Marcus has to give us a frame. How can we set any marks? Come on, Andrea, this is ridiculous. It's Filmmaking 101! *(The intercom buzzes.)*

ANDREA. Just do what you can, guys, please ... *(Andrea exits.)*

DAVE. Let's line the thing up.

OSCAR. I got it. *(Oscar moves the rig to camera.)*

DAVE. *(To Ron.)* Can you give me a hero?

RON. *(Crossing to the cooler by the prop table.)* I got a stand-in.

DAVE. Go in on the mag.

OSCAR. On the mag.

DAVE. Good. Hold that. That seems right.

OSCAR. He said he wanted to be tight on a low angle — you know, like lookin' up at it.

DAVE. We need to be higher, Ron, grab a couple apple boxes.

OSCAR. I got 'em. *(Ron lifts the rig as Oscar positions the apple boxes.)*

DAVE. Next side up. *(As Oscar adjusts the apple boxes, Dave angles the camera.)* Let me just tilt.

OSCAR. How's it look? *(Dave looks through the camera and points a flashlight at the hero cup.)*

DAVE. *(Behind the eyepiece.)* Good. Really. Very good.

OSCAR. Lemme set this key light.

JEFFREY. *(Examining the swirl.)* What is this stuff anyway?

RON. It's the hero. Except by the time we shoot it'll probably be a little old and I'll have to make up a new one. So it's the stand-in, I guess, if you want to split hairs.

JEFFREY. This isn't the product, is it? The stuff they sent wouldn't hold up like this. Something's different.

DAVE. Back off, Jeffrey.

JEFFREY. What is it?

RON. Nothing special ...

JEFFREY. Shaving cream?

RON. And food coloring ... and three teaspoons of cornstarch ... and two level tablespoons of confectioners' sugar ... and some stuff I can't even begin to talk about.

JEFFREY. Ron! You wanna get us all sued? This is a product launch for a major national chain. Have you ever heard of a legal department? Corporations have these things called legal departments.

RON. Hey, hey. Take a deep breath. It's not like I'm trying to pull a fast one. It's up to the man. Everything's always up to the man. I just know that all I heard here Friday was: "Why can't we make it more fuckin' creamy?" So, you know, here's creamy!

OSCAR. It won't melt in the light?

RON. Nope.

OSCAR. Gonna save us a lot of downtime.

RON. It holds for a whole half hour. I tested it. This is what he wants, Oscar: This is Chicago.

OSCAR. Could be good ...

JEFFREY. Who is gonna tell him?

OSCAR. Don't tell him. Tell Andrea. Let Andrea tell him.

JEFFREY. We'll be back to square one — *(Andre enters and crosses upstage.)*

ANDREA. I'm sorry, it's gonna be a few more minutes. There's nothing I can do. He didn't expect to be shooting today.

RON. We're working things out on our own.

JEFFREY. Tell her.

ANDREA. What?

JEFFREY. Now.

OSCAR. Simmer down, Jeffrey.

ANDREA. Tell me what?

JEFFREY. The swirl.

ANDREA. I showed him. He likes it. It's fine.

RON. Terrific.

JEFFREY. Ron.

ANDREA. What?

RON. It's ... a variation.

ANDREA. A what?

JEFFREY. It's shaving cream.

ANDREA. You're kidding.

JEFFREY. He's not kidding.

ANDREA. Marcus approved it.

JEFFREY. *(To Ron.)* I told you.

ANDREA. Now I gotta tell him it's shaving cream?

RON. Well, it's creamy.

ANDREA. Jeffrey ...

JEFFREY. We'll use what I froze on Friday.

ANDREA. Can you try something else?

JEFFREY. Not now. Not with no notice. It wouldn't look too good —

ANDREA. This is not what I need. Listen, the longer he's on this conference call, the sharper his teeth are gonna be when he gets back here. Just stay on set. That's all I ask. *(Andrea exits. Ron sits on the sofa. Jeffrey takes the hero swirl to the freezer and removes his own hero, a pathetic nothing compared to Ron's creation. Dave crosses to the food table and slowly peels a Hershey's Kiss.)*

DAVE. Tension and boredom. *(Beat.)* Coffee and sugary snacks. *(Beat.)* No music, no natural light. No phone calls. No routine. No predictability. Just fear and panic. Panic and fear.

RON. Wow!

OSCAR. What?

RON. I just remembered this totally bizarre thing.

DAVE. What?

RON. When I was in France. Katie made this reservation at this bed and breakfast on this sheep farm near Toulouse. Actually, it wasn't near Toulouse. It wasn't near anything. Which was why Katie wanted to go there. To get away.

JEFFREY. Ron, nobody cares.

RON. And I was jet-lagged and I got lost and I had a little fender bender in the rental car and the guy I hit was really nice about the whole thing, but we had to fill out this accident report, in French, of course, duh, and there was this greasy little local police officer and his breath stank of garlic and duck liver ...

JEFFREY. Ron!

RON. Okay, so by the time I got to this farm, I was extremely tired. I mean, I was as tired as I have ever been in my life. Only the problem is the room that we have in this bed and breakfast — I don't know if this is because of sheep shit or what — it's full of flies. But I don't care. I am so frigging tired. I fall facedown on the pillow and I'm gone. And Katie's still puttering around and unpacking her underwear, but I'm out cold. Deep, regular breathing. And then suddenly I hear this "bzzzsch, bzzzsch" inside my head. There's this sound inside my head. And I wake up and I stagger around with probably like a folded cotton imprint in my cheek — you know, like you get? — and I turn to Katie and I say, "Something is alive inside my head." And she's like, "Right." You know, "You're dreaming, dear." And I hear this "bzzzsch, bzzzsch" right there inside my brain. And she can't hear it. But she sees the fear in my eyes, and it hits me: A FLY HAS CRAWLED INSIDE MY EAR. So I go, "Katie, Katie, look in my ear. Can you see anything?" And she's like, "Nooo." And now I'm hearing this "Pchchi, pch-chi, pch-chi" which I somehow know to be the sound of those tiny fly pincers on the tiny fly face that's shoved up against my eardrum — you know, how they're supposed to throw up and eat their vomit or whatever. So I go completely apeshit. What am I gonna do? Drive to a hospital? There is no hospital. I mean this part of France is so in the middle of nowhere the French air force makes sonic booms over it. It's all dirt farms and dirt roads and little stone huts and I'm panicking. And Katie's panicking. She's also like laughing a little bit, which is really pissing me off. So I'm listening to this "bzzzsch" and this "ph-chi, ph-chi, ph-chi." I can't even express the *clarity* of this sound. And I'm jamming my pinky in my ear and crying and panting and pacing. And then Katie gets the idea, brilliant idea, "We can drown it." So I like hold my head under this faucet and she turns on the water and now I'm hearing this submarine "bzzzsch, bzzzsch" and this underwater "pcch-chi, pcch-chi." And I just stay there with my head under the tap and it's amazing. I listen to this fly's agony. "Bzzzzzzzzssssschhhh,

61

bzzzzzzzssssschhhh, bzzzzzzzsssssschhhhhhhhhhhhhhhhh." I hear it slowly die. *(Beat.)* And I get up and I towel off and I go back to bed thinking about this little dead creature nestled there next to my brain.

JEFFREY. Thank you, Ron.

RON. And, I swear, that's how I feel when I'm here. I'm like that fly. I crawled someplace warm and it seemed really very interesting at first, but now it's like I'm stuck. I shoulda' found something at least three-eighths.

JEFFREY. Ron, I gotta tell you, if you take that thing apart, the man's gonna go ballistic.

RON. I'm just thinking ...

JEFFREY. What?

RON. The setup's fine: It's got the extra axis.

JEFFREY. *(To the others.)* He's talking to himself again.

RON. It's just, you know, sometimes he's just looking for something to shoot down. So maybe I should use a thicker shaft here and a better coupling and a bigger platter. Just for eyewash.

JEFFREY. What's this?

RON. That's a limit switch. There's one on the bottom here too. So you can set a stop mark. See?

JEFFREY. So you just slide it along this tubing and lock it with this set screw?

RON. And I've got the Allen wrench taped right here. Nice and handy. These are both Bodine motors. DC, variable speed.

JEFFREY. Smooth.

RON. Very smooth. I just underbuilt it up top. Look, I've gotta get to work.

JEFFREY. You want him to walk in and see you bent over this thing?

RON. No.

JEFFREY. You said you were ready.

RON. I just want to go in the back and put together like a little safety kit. In case he wants to beef it up. I want to prepare for the worst, okay? Cover me. Back in five. Less than five. *(Ron exits and everyone waits a moment.)*

JEFFREY. He couldn't find his dick with a flashlight.

DAVE. Help him out.

JEFFREY. What am I gonna do?

DAVE. Go back there.

JEFFREY. What's the point?

DAVE. *(Looking at Ron's rig.)* Is this thing even gonna work?

JEFFREY. We'll see.

OSCAR. It probably will. Just leave it alone.

JEFFREY. Doesn't really matter.

DAVE. He'll hate it.

JEFFREY. He'll find a way to hate it.

DAVE. Just another day picking the legs off a grasshopper. *(Ron shouts from the offstage shop.)*

RON. Where's the drill rod?

JEFFREY. *(So Ron can hear him.)* In the bin.

RON. There isn't any.

JEFFREY. I used it on those taco slides.

RON. All of it?

JEFFREY. Yeah, pretty much. *(Ron enters, confused.)*

RON. Why didn't you tell me?

JEFFREY. Don't you do an inventory?

RON. I never remember.

JEFFREY. So remember.

RON. I have a hard job, Jeffrey.

JEFFREY. Yes. You do, Ron. You have a hard job at which you sort of suck.

RON. I don't expect someone to use twelve pieces of three-eighths shaft and not let me know.

JEFFREY. So scavenge something.

RON. I need help.

JEFFREY. No chance.

RON. Please, Jeffrey, I'm in trouble.

DAVE. Come on, Jeffrey.

JEFFREY. Andrea wants us to stay on set.

DAVE. Nobody's coming. We can cover.

JEFFREY. Famous last words.

DAVE. Go back there.

OSCAR. Stay out of it.

DAVE. You stay out of it.

OSCAR. No, YOU stay out of it.

JEFFREY. Fine.

RON. Thank you, Jeffrey.

JEFFREY. Fuck you, Ron. *(Dave watches as Ron follows Jeffrey off-stage.)*

DAVE. I admire Ron. I do. He is what he is.

OSCAR. You like that?

DAVE. Yes, I do.

OSCAR. Dave, you're gay, aren't you?

DAVE. Oscar, you're black, aren't you?

OSCAR. I don't hide it.

DAVE. Look, I don't lie, Oscar, I just don't tell the truth. Can you name one guy, I mean, you know, not hair-and-makeup or wardrobe, one real crew member who is openly gay?

OSCAR. Not on commercials.

DAVE. It's not allowed.

OSCAR. I get you. Yeah, there's plenty of air in the closet, right? Not a lot of light, but plenty of air. And you got that nice pile of old coats in the corner to curl up in.

DAVE. Who are you to talk — with your nice Tidy-Bowl-Man fuckin'-PG-13 version of a black man?

OSCAR. Dave, I wanted to ask you something. Did you ever think that if the two of us opened that store, selling pipe fittings and hand tools and all, you know, most of our customers were gonna be —

DAVE. Men. Yes, Oscar. I'd sort of scoped that out on my own. I like to work those hardware stores. Great place to pick up dates.

OSCAR. You don't need that anymore, do you? You got a new boyfriend … *(Jeffrey returns.)*

JEFFREY. I've had it, man, I wash my hands. Ron's gone, went down the service elevator. He's gonna go over to Harris Hardware.

DAVE. What for?

JEFFREY. Drill rod and shaft collars and God knows what.

DAVE. Couldn't you cut up one of your rigs?

JEFFREY. They're all welded.

DAVE. You could pull out the PortaBand.

JEFFREY. I don't feel like it, okay? This is Ron's rig. Let Ron fix it. *(Andrea enters and everyone scrambles.)*

ANDREA. Okay, here we go. Oscar, by the way, it's done. Marcus said to tell you, you've got a deal.

OSCAR. Just like that?

ANDREA. We talked to the realtor, faxed the paperwork — I'm telling you, it's done. *(Marcus enters, eyes down on a Palm Pilot.)*

MARCUS. *(Ominously.)* Dave.

DAVE. Yes, sir.

MARCUS. I hear you won't be with us on Friday.

DAVE. No, I can't.

MARCUS. Why not?

DAVE. I told Andrea.

MARCUS. It's something personal.

DAVE. Yes it is.

MARCUS. Oh, personal. What's personal? Tell me, Dave.

DAVE. I put a guy on hold for you.

MARCUS. No, we're fine; we don't need your help.

DAVE. Look, Marcus, maybe I can work something out ...

MARCUS. Are we ready?

OSCAR. Marcus, I just wanted to say thank you, sir.

MARCUS. *(With a handshake.)* It's a pleasure. You're my partner. I'm glad to do it. *(The intercom beeps.)*

MARCUS. Kill it. Kill the intercom. Could you kill the fucking intercom? Andrea, I told the girl. I can't have any interruptions!

ANDREA. Jerry Golding on three. *(Marcus crosses and picks up the phone.)*

MARCUS. Hey.

ANDREA. *(To the crew.)* Stand by, guys, we'll be ready shortly.

MARCUS. *(To Jerry.)* No. Not yet. But we worked it all out. No, I know. I know value. I remember value. *(Beat.)* I said I'd try. I told you I'd try. Hey. Hey, now, wait a minute. I'm busting my nuts for you. I'm doing everything I can ... *(Beat.)* No, Jerry, there is no other guy. I'm your guy. I'm your guy on Breyers. You know my reel. My ice cream reel. Nobody can touch that. Nobody even comes close, my friend. *(Beat.)* Look, I gotta go now. I gotta get to work. I got some shit I gotta shoot for free. *(Marcus hangs up and looks to his crew.)* Whose turn is it to fuck me now?

ANDREA. Heat 'em up.

OSCAR. *(Throwing the bull switch.)* Watch your eyes.

ANDREA. Here we go.

JEFFREY. Standing by.

65

DAVE. Standing by.

ANDREA. Everything clean?

MARCUS. Open up a second.

DAVE. Wide open.

MARCUS. Stop down.

DAVE. Stopping down.

ANDREA. Ready, Jeffrey?

JEFFREY. Standing by.

ANDREA. Roll tape.

OSCAR. Tape speed.

ANDREA. Camera. *(The camera revs.)*

DAVE. SPEED! *(Jeffrey competently pours the liquid.)*

MARCUS. CUT! Check the gate. We're moving on.

OSCAR. Playback?

MARCUS. I said we're moving on. Where's my turntable? Where's my swirl? *(Oscar throws the bull switch. Everyone stops, knowing what's coming. Then Andrea turns to Marcus.)*

ANDREA. We've got a small problem.

MARCUS. What?

ANDREA. The swirl that you saw won't work for the takes.

MARCUS. I loved it. It was perfect. What're you talkin'?

JEFFREY. It's shaving cream.

ANDREA. It was a mistake. We still have the heros from last week. We'll be fine.

MARCUS. We're not fine. We are not fucking fine. What the fuck is happening?

ANDREA. Marcus —

MARCUS. Where is it?

ANDREA. It doesn't matter.

MARCUS. Just give it to me.

ANDREA. Give it to him, Jeffrey. *(As Jeffrey goes to get Ron's hero from the freezer, Ron enters, breathless, carrying a paper bag.)*

RON. I was on a run. I'm sorry. I got what we need.

MARCUS. What is this?

RON. Oh. Um. A vertical axis.

MARCUS. A what?

RON. It's an option.

MARCUS. I wanted a turntable, a simple, silly turntable.

JEFFREY. Not a problem.

ANDREA. It's standing by.

MARCUS. Gimme some light. Let's run the piece of shit. See if it falls apart.

DAVE. The gate's good. *(Oscar turn on a light on the setup stage left. Ron and Jeffrey pick up motor controllers. Dave crosses to the Mitchell camera.)*

ANDREA. On your switches.

JEFFREY. Standing by.

RON. Can I please just catch my breath?

MARCUS. Jeffrey, you move the cup into frame. My cue. The other guy just rotates. You got marks? You ready, Jeffrey?

RON. Hold on.

JEFFREY. Set.

RON. No.

MARCUS. What do you mean, "no"?

RON. I never set a position.

MARCUS. You told them to rehearse?

ANDREA. Yes, I did.

RON. We were waiting for you.

MARCUS. Get a mark. Just get a goddamn start mark. This. Okay? This is your mark!

RON. *(Under the rig.)* Marking.

MARCUS. Help him, Jeffrey. Hire the handicapped. This is asinine.

RON. I'm on it. I'm okay. Standing by.

ANDREA. Rehearsal. Ready.

MARCUS. And action. *(Ron and Jeffrey operate controllers.)* Okay.

OSCAR. Oh, that's nice …

MARCUS. It isn't bad.

JEFFREY. You want to give me an end mark?

MARCUS. No. This is beautiful. Just keep moving it through. Good. Okay. And … cut. *(Turning.)* Did you get that, Oscar?

OSCAR. Got it.

MARCUS. I like this. I like it. I like how it looks.

ANDREA. I'm glad.

JEFFREY. But you can't use the shaving cream.

MARCUS. It's a two-second shot. Nobody's gonna know. You gotta see it in this lens — it's fuckin' gorgeous.

JEFFREY. But, what ... what if they ... find out?

MARCUS. How could they? Are you gonna tell 'em? They just want what they want, Jeffrey.

JEFFREY. Ethics in Advertising —

MARCUS. Ho. Stop. That's enough, son. Let's just get it in the can.

RON. He likes it.

MARCUS. What?

RON. Nothing.

MARCUS. I'm gonna need a focus pull.

DAVE. You want me to measure?

MARCUS. Later. I wanna watch it. Let's go again.

ANDREA. Right away, back to one.

JEFFREY. Going to one.

ANDREA. Ron?

RON. Sorry.

JEFFREY. That's *not* the start mark.

RON. Sorry.

JEFFREY. Standing by.

MARCUS. Andrea.

ANDREA. Come on, guys. *(Ron struggles with his switch.)*

MARCUS. Let's go now.

ANDREA. On the rehearsal, and, ready, and ...

MARCUS. Action. *(Ron rotates the cup in the wrong direction.)*

MARCUS. No! You go clock. You go clockwise. How we gonna read the logo? Andrea, I don't have time for this.

ANDREA. Back to one.

RON. Back to one.

MARCUS. Get it right.

ANDREA. Ready?

JEFFREY. Ready.

RON. Ready.

ANDREA. Rehearsal. Your cue, Marcus. Call it.

MARCUS. And ACTION. *(Ron and Jeffrey start the move.)* Oh, Jesus, that's pretty. Oh yes. Go slower on the rotation. Down a point.

RON. On the rotation.

MARCUS. Just like that. Yes. Yes.

RON. Okay!

MARCUS. You're good there. Oh, oh. And ... cut.

ANDREA. You want to get it on film?

MARCUS. Not yet. Oscar, gimme a white card on the bottom — two-inch by ten-inch strip. We're on our game now, fellas —

RON. Should Jeffrey change his start mark?

MARCUS. What?

RON. If you change speeds, that should change the start mark. Wasn't that the whole idea? That the lift and the spin should happen together? *(Words fail Marcus.)*

ANDREA. Ron, Marcus directs. You flip the switch. Just flip the switch. *(Oscar positions a stand with a white card.)*

MARCUS. Drop it there, Oscar; let's do the move.

DAVE. Take it easy.

RON. I'm trying ... *(Ron begins to laugh involuntarily.)* ... and failing.

MARCUS. Think that's funny?

RON. No.

MARCUS. You having fun?

RON. No.

MARCUS. You get some kind of kick out of wasting my time?

RON. No, sir.

MARCUS. Good, Oscar. Closer. Good. Okay. Walk away. *(Oscar crosses to operate video.)*

ANDREA. Here we go.

MARCUS. Open up.

DAVE. Wide open. *(Ron flips on his motor controller.)*

MARCUS. What're you doing?

RON. I'm —

MARCUS. What are you fucking doing?

RON. I'm setting a speed.

MARCUS. You're what?

RON. It won't happen again.

MARCUS. But it will. It does. It happens again and again all day long. You treat this like a fucking lesson at the Learning Lab. This is a job!

RON. I know.

MARCUS. You get in my way.

RON. That's not my intention.

MARCUS. Fuck your intention! Rotate the cup. On cue. Practice the rotation when I'm in my office. That's your intention.

RON. Yes, sir.

ANDREA. Here we go.

MARCUS. *(To Dave.)* That's the focus.

DAVE. Got it.

MARCUS. Now go back to one and just do what I say. You understand? Just ... what ... I ... fucking ... say.

ANDREA. Roll tape.

OSCAR. Tape speed. *(Ron hits his switch early.)*

MARCUS. Jesus fuck!

RON. God.

DAVE. Calm down.

RON. I can't.

MARCUS. You can't?!

RON. Would you give me a second here, please? *(Ron stands, retreats to a corner and takes a few deep breaths, his back to Marcus. Marcus just watches. He can't believe what he's seeing.)*

MARCUS. Take all the time you want.

RON. I just need a second.

MARCUS. Take a week.

RON. I'm sorry.

MARCUS. Take a month.

RON. I'm sorry.

MARCUS. You're fired.

RON. I'm sorry.

ANDREA. Marcus —

MARCUS. I said you're fired. Talk to Andrea. Call her tomorrow. Oscar, cool the light. Jeffrey, I need you to fix this thing.

JEFFREY. Yes, sir.

MARCUS. I'm gonna keep this motor at the bottom. You just gotta make it more solid up in here. Maybe a thicker piece of drill rod.

JEFFREY. Three-eighths.

MARCUS. Exactly.

JEFFREY. *(Opening the paper bag that Ron brought in.)* We can do that.

MARCUS. Get one of the good couplings, a bigger platter. I don't know where he dug up this wanky piece of shit. The configuration's fine.

70

JEFFREY. Right.

MARCUS. You need a little time?

JEFFREY. Not much. *(Jeffrey goes right to work. Ron remains frozen.)*

MARCUS. I like it real tight with the wide-angle here.

DAVE. Uh-huh.

MARCUS. Oscar ...

OSCAR. Yes, sir.

MARCUS. Hit it with a hard light.

OSCAR. A hard light?

MARCUS. Take that baby, rake it across the top.

OSCAR. Okay. *(Marcus notices Ron standing motionless.)*

MARCUS. What's with him? What's he got, a screw loose? Andrea, talk to him.

ANDREA. Ron, pack your tools and get out.

MARCUS. Is this kid a head case or what?

ANDREA. I said OUT! *(After a long look to Andrea, Ron crosses to the worktable, picks up a briefcase-sized tool case and exits up right.)*

MARCUS. *(To Oscar at the video cart.)* Flag that off the cup. *(Marcus crosses to the phone, dials and gets a receptionist. Into the phone:)* Gimme Jerry Golding. Marcus. Marcus Gordon. *(To Golding now.)* Jerry, listen. Wait. Stop. Hold it. I have news. I have very good news. You know how you wanted something extra on that move? Right. In twenty three. Listen. I got it. I got it for you. I got this little up-from-below thing. *(Beat.)* It's dramatic. Very dramatic. And here's the kicker, buddy: I got that swirl. *(Beat.)* Oh, is it ever. This is gonna make Dairy Queen look like fuckin' dog shit, Jerry. You're gonna win an award for this. *(Beat.)* Oh, yeah, easy. Not a problem. It's at the lab in an hour. *(Barking at Oscar for effect.)* Kill that par back there; it's too much.

OSCAR. Killing.

MARCUS. *(Back to the phone.)* You know what, Jerry? I'm not even thinking about Breyers. I don't even care about it anymore. I'm having too much fun! *(Hearing bad news.)* Come over now? Why would you? I'll be done by the time you get here. *(Marcus is rattled. Andrea crosses to him and silently waves, trying to prevent the inevitable.)* No, I'm not gonna stop you. If you want to come you can come. Okay. So. We'll see you. *(Marcus hangs up the phone.)*

ANDREA. You can't let him come over here.

MARCUS. Well, he is.

ANDREA. I could call.

MARCUS. It's too late.

ANDREA. You should have said no.

MARCUS. Well, I didn't. So let's go; let's start shooting. You ready, Jeffrey? *(Ron enters carrying a canvas bag in one hand and his briefcase-sized case in the other.)*

RON. I'd like to say something.

MARCUS. Andrea.

ANDREA. Lemme handle it.

JEFFREY. Ron —

ANDREA. Please.

RON. I'm leaving. I'm leaving, okay? But I did really want to mention to Marcus how much I admire him. I mean this. I do. I admire Marcus. I admire the way he runs this business.

JEFFREY. When are you gonna learn to shut your mouth?

RON. It's the truth. I tell people. I talk about Marcus all the time.

JEFFREY. Ron, what are you doing?

RON. *(Dropping his bags loudly to the floor.)* What are *you* doing, Jeffrey? You're just bullshit. You're all bullshit. I can count the ways. Jeffrey's a thief. Andrea's a whore. Dave's a coward. Oscar's a slave. Ah, but everyone's a slave to Marcus. Except for me. Because I don't work here anymore.

ANDREA. Enough!

MARCUS. You're a nobody. You're nothing —

ANDREA. Ron. Hey. You've got to go now. *(When Andrea reaches for him, Ron recoils.)*

MARCUS. Wait. What he wants is attention. So let's just stand here and watch him 'til he's gone. *(Marcus approaches Ron with exaggerated calm, like an orderly in a mental ward.)* Okay, now, kid, here's the deal. We've got work to do and you're in our way. It's a little embarrassing. I mean, for you. To be all upset here. So why don't you just wipe up your tears and pick up your bag and go along home and let the rest of us get on with what we have to do. You can call Andrea tomorrow and she can send you your check. How's that sound? Is that good for you?

RON. *(Dead.)* Sure.

MARCUS. Get out of my shop. *(As Marcus and the crew go back*

72

to work, Ron picks up his bags and starts to skulk off. When he's about to pass the set, Ron stops, drops his bags, yanks the hero cup from the rig and scrambles up the ladder by the mountain of fruit. He lifts the cup high in the air.)

ANDREA. Ron.

OSCAR. Ron.

DAVE. Ron.

MARCUS. Fuck.

JEFFREY. Give it back.

ANDREA. Please.

RON. This is mine. I made it. Didn't I, Jeffrey? So what's the problem? Jeffrey can make you another one, Marcus. Can't you, Jeffrey? Wait, but what were those ingredients again? Can he do what I did with the spatula? Did Jeffrey ever study any Chinese calligraphy?

JEFFREY. You little faggot.

MARCUS. Shut up, Jeffrey. Now listen, kid. Listen to me. That's your work. You want a little appreciation. You want a better chance. We can talk about that.

RON. Oh, can we?

ANDREA. Marcus, you can't.

MARCUS. I have got six minutes to get this shot!

RON. But the hero's up here.

JEFFREY. Fuckin' kill him.

MARCUS. Shut the fuck up, you little fuck!!!

RON. Hey, how's it feel, Jeffrey?

MARCUS. Let's be reasonable, kid. The client's coming. My back's to the wall. What do you want? You wanna do props here?

RON. I've *been* doing props here.

MARCUS. You want credit?

RON. I want respect.

MARCUS. *(Wincing.)* Nnn. Can't help you there. That's not on the menu.

RON. Okay. I want work. That's all I ever wanted.

MARCUS. You got it. You're the prop. Starting right now.

RON. Whoa.

DAVE. Oh man …

RON. Are you serious?

ANDREA. *(Taking Marcus aside.)* Marcus, you are aware that Jeffrey could file a grievance …

MARCUS. Then let him.

ANDREA. You can't just hand out union work.

MARCUS. I got a shot to get, Andrea. What's my choice? I GOT NO GODDAMN CHOICE!!!

ANDREA. This is wrong. Your whole crew could walk. Their Local could come in and shut you down. *(Marcus crosses to Dave and Oscar.)* Don't do this, I'm telling you. There's a precedent. It has happened.

MARCUS. What do you say, fellas? Oscar? Dave? You hear her? You know I need this. I need it. You're my guys. I need you. You wanna walk, you can walk. Just say so. Say the word. *(Oscar and Dave remain silent. To Andrea:)* You see that? *(Ron begins carefully backing down the ladder. He gingerly holds the hero cup away from his body. All eyes are on him and he knows it.)*

RON. Okay, Oscar, could you spot me here please? *(Oscar crosses and clears the way for Ron, who approaches the set, carefully cradling the hero.)* Dave, I need you to smooth that adhesive for me. Just press it down with your thumbs if you can. Great. Perfect. I'll get a rough lock and then finesse it at the eyepiece. Right where we were before. Oscar, give me the soft light. Dave, the inclinometer.

DAVE. I've got it. *(Dave hands Ron a tool. Oscar switches on the set lights. Ron turns on the vertical axis motor and checks the cup's orientation.)*

RON. Thank you, David. Okay, Marcus, we'll be ready in just a moment. I want to check for fingerprints and get a new mark here and then I can line up on the crosshairs for you. We don't have a lot of time on this hero. It's gonna go lacy. We should shoot the rehearsal. *(Ron confidently climbs onto the dolly, looks in the eyepiece, then picks up the motor controller to check its setting.)* All right, we're good on the level and good in the lens. I'm gonna need some help with the other controller. *(In a single swift movement, Marcus grabs Ron's ear and pulls him across the room.)*

MARCUS. You pompous brat —

DAVE. Do something, Oscar.

MARCUS. *(Doubling Ron over.)* You gotta lotta damn gall.

OSCAR. Marcus —

MARCUS. You stay out!

OSCAR. Come on, now. *(Marcus grabs and brandishes a large plastic cooler, fending Oscar off.)*

MARCUS. It's my business. You're a bid-niz-man now, aren't you? You oughta know.

DAVE. Oscar —

MARCUS. I'm helping him. I'm teaching him the rule. The one rule. You work *for* me, son. You don't work *with* me. You get that? You got that? What's so hard about that?

RON. Nothing.

DAVE. Let him go.

MARCUS. *(Twisting Ron's ear.)* You understand me?

RON. Yes.

MARCUS. I don't think you do.

DAVE. Stop it.

RON. OWWW!

DAVE. Stop him.

MARCUS. We don't need another director. *(Ron pulls free.)*

RON. I DON'T NEED ANOTHER DADDY!

MARCUS. *(Swinging the cooler at Ron.)* YOU SNOT-NOSED CUNT!!! *(Oscar intercepts the cooler and struggles with Marcus in a pathetic tug-of-war, which ends with Marcus losing balance and falling into his own set, toppling the table and sending wood and fruit clattering and bouncing to the floor.)*

RON. *(Clutching his ear.)* You're sick, man ...

MARCUS. Jeffrey ...

RON. You're a mess.

MARCUS. *(Struggling awkwardly to his feet.)* Yeah? Look who's talking. I need help over here.

RON. Look at you — you're pathetic.

MARCUS. Jeffrey ...

RON. *(Overlapping.)* You're phoning it in, Marcus — you haven't had an original idea in years.

MARCUS. *(Overlapping and crossing to camera.)* Let's go, Jeffrey. You're the one. Let's shoot this. Andrea, you take the other box. Okay, fellas, here we go.

RON. *(Overlapping.)* And you know it, don't you? Key from the left, fill from the right, card on the bottom, eight-eleven split: it's a formula. It's the same, the same every time.

MARCUS. *(Still overlapping, reaching a peak.)* Andrea ... Andrea ... Andrea, are you with me?

ANDREA. No!

MARCUS. What do you mean, "No"?

ANDREA. *(Crossing to camera.)* This is unacceptable.

MARCUS. What is?

ANDREA. All of it.

MARCUS. What are you talking about?

ANDREA. It's gone lacy.

MARCUS. Andrea, it's all I've got!

ANDREA. *(Picking up the hero cup.)* Is it? *(Andrea flings the cup to the floor. Splat! Marcus falls to his knees and reaches for his ruined hero.)*

MARCUS. No! No! No! *(Marcus tries in vain to scoop the pink crap back into the cup, then collapses, sobbing. The intercom buzzes. Andrea stays calm.)*

ANDREA. Gentlemen, let's start again; we need a new hero.

JEFFREY. Ron, what can I do?

RON. Get the whisk. *(The intercom buzzes again, and all at once, Ron, Jeffrey, Dave and Oscar swing into action, leaving Marcus down on the floor.)*

OSCAR. I'll get the mop.

JEFFREY. The whisk's here.

DAVE. I've got a card. *(The intercom buzzes once more and Andrea crosses to pick up the phone. Andrea and the crew ad-lib and overlap through the following.)*

RON. Get the cornstarch. In the kitchen. On the counter. By the coffee. And confectioners' sugar. Oh, and the food coloring. It's over there. On the table.

ANDREA. *(To the receptionist.)* Put him on. *(To Golding now.)* Jerry. It's about time you got here! Where you been? We've been waiting.

JEFFREY. Okay, what else?

ANDREA. *(With a laugh.)* Kidding. Kidding. I'm kidding kiddo.

RON. The fake ice from Trengove. The stuff that we used on the beer bottles. It's in my canvas bag over there in a salt shaker with a piece of red electrical tape on top.

ANDREA. *(To the crew.)* Sssshhh! *(Back to Jerry, and we hear her better now.)* We're just tweaking. You didn't miss a thing. You're perfect, Jerry, as always.

OSCAR. *(To Dave.)* I'll be right over there.

RON. A little water.

JEFFREY. It'll be cold.

ANDREA. No, don't move. I'll come and get you. Be right out. *(Andrea hangs up and exits as the crew continues to work. Marcus stands and tries to clean himself with a paper towel. Oscar is trying to mop up the mess, and Marcus is in his way.)*

MARCUS. *(Feeling Oscar's stare.)* What? What are you lookin' at? Get back to work.

RON. Get back to work *please. (Marcus just stops. Then he begins to laugh at the absurdity of the moment. His employees, however, are not laughing. They also aren't moving. Marcus looks over to Jeffrey and Ron: nothing. To Dave: motionless. He turns to Oscar, and Oscar just folds his big hands over the top of his mop and waits. It dawns on Marcus: It's his move.)*

MARCUS. *(Barely able to say the words.)* Get back to work ... p ... p ... *(Especially this one.)* ... please. *(Work resumes and Marcus heads up to his office. Fade to black.)*

End of Play

PROPERTY LIST AND SET PRESETS

The play's maiden production was realistic to an extreme. It involved something like fourteen tons of real equipment, only a fraction of which is listed here. Because of my work in the film industry, I was able to get a lot of stuff from friends and suppliers. That's not the only way to go. The play's action and dialogue make most sense if the characters stay pretty busy cleaning fruit, positioning lights, fussing with cameras. I leave the extent and specifics of their business up to you.

—R.A.

OFFSTAGE LEFT
Dave's shoulder bag (blue)
2 Chap Sticks in webbed zipper pouch
Date book
LOA envelope in rear pocket
Jeffrey's bag (black)
Venti Starbucks cup with coffee
Junk mail
Chicago reel in FedEx envelope
Paper bag with box of cornstarch with empty soda bottle
Green-lidded Tupperware
AdWeek magazine
Paper bag with $3/_8$-inch drill rod
Water pitcher withwater
Water cups
Box of Kleenex

OFFSTAGE DOWN LEFT
Damp mop
Backup motor power cable in elevator

OFFSTAGE LEFT IN "SHOP"
Spyder dolly with legs folded in
Steering wheel with dolly
Black box with Mitchell camera with lens cap

Red box with friction head
5K with cable coiled
Motor controller for Ron's rig
Can of Dust Off

STAGE LEFT WORK TABLE
ON TABLE:
　　Small cooler with hero U.L.
　　Jeffrey's toolbox (open) D.R.
　　Ron's toolbox U.R.
　　Polaroid of fruit on Jeffrey's box
　　5 pieces of duvateen on Jeffrey's box
　　Can of WD-40 behind Ron's box on its side
　　Coiled piece of silver armature wire
　　Short arm with white card
　　Daily News
　　Camara lens with lens caps
　　Large camera mag S.L.
　　Small camera mag S.L.
　　Gray pouch with lens spray and cloth
　　Assorted markers
　　Sheet of logos
UNDER TABLE:
　　Can of shaving cream S.L.
　　2 apple boxes on end S.R.
　　1 apple box on side S.R.
　　Brown milk crate with blocks
　　2 open rolls paper towels — U.S.
　　1 roll unopened S.L.

STAGE LEFT
Video cart with ³/₄-inch video deck
Pen and paper
Oscar's glasses
Videocassette in video deck's mouth
Remote
Apple box at cart
4 C-stands S.L. of cart (in groups of two)

Power cable for Ron's rig
Power cable for 2K S.R. of rig cable
Power cable for second rig motor under Ceco cart
3 sandbags at D.S. end of blue cart
Spyder dolly head on low shelf
Handtruck at elevator

KITCHEN
FRIDGE:
    Blue-lidded Tupperware with salad
    Bag of baby carrots
FRIDGE DOOR:
    Miscellaneous dressing
FREEZER:
    Jeffrey's hero
U.S. COUNTER:
    Knife block
    Knife in block
    Handi-cloth in sink on divider
    Salad dressing bottle S.L. of sink
    Coffeemaker with coffee — fresh
    Box of food coloring with red bottle
    2 rolls of paper towels
    Boxes of Ziploc bags, garbage bags
    Strawberry cutting board
    Pitcher of water
    Stack of cups
    Miscellaneous kitchen stuff S.L. of sink
    3 stools S.L.
    Garbage can D. withextra bag tied to handle
    Rolling stand S.L. of garbage can
    1 baby stand S.L. of garbage can
    1 Silver C-stand S.L. of garbage can

UPSTAGE
Black sofa
End table S.L.
Lamp on end table — on

Tchotchke U.S. of lamp
Coffee table D. of sofa
Phone S.R. on coffee table
3 magazines S.L. on coffee table

CENTER STAGE
Moviola dolly set in to table
Camera on dolly with lens cap
Dave's camera bag on dolly
IN BAG:
    Tape measure
    Mini-maglite
    Light motor
TABLETOP:
    Sawhorses on green spikes
    Tabletop, square and flush with D. edges of saw horse
    Fruit stand
    Fruit (see Polaroids)
    Plastic tarp over fruit — covered D. and centered
    Inky with snoot U.R.
    Baby with diffusion D.R.
    Tall Baby O.L.
    Tweenie S.L.
    Flag D.L.
    10K S.L.
    White card U.L. — in to fruit
    Sandbags on all stands except 10K
    Good stage box under S.R. sawhorse
    Bad stage box D. of 10K
    Yellow 4-step ladder S.R.

ROAD BOX
JEFFREY'S TOOL BELT:
    Large tweezers
    Grease pencil
2 sandbags under box
Roll of black wrap in box — pre-snipped
Apple box D. of box

Toolbox with S.L. side open on apple box
Q-tips in toolbox
Green floral wire in toolbox
Thumbtacks in toolbox
Water bucket S.R. — $1/_4$ to $1/_2$ full
Slop bucket S.R. — open
Cooler with 3 bags of "fruit freeze" mixture
1 bag of mixture prepped to spill
ON ROAD BOX:
> Spritz bottle with water
> Small roll of paper towels on arm D.R.
> Strip of paper towels laid out U.S. on box
> White mixing bowl — S.R.
> Whisk in bowl
> Pink pitcher hung on S.R. side — U.S.
> Blue pitcher hung on S.R. side — D.
> 3 hero cups — D.L.
> 1 red marker set in tape roll
> 1 roll 2-inch black gaff — bottom
> 1 roll 2-inch gray gaff — mid
> 1 roll 1-inch white gaff — top
> Trash bag on S.L. side

CRAFT SERVICES
Practical light D. — switched off
Stage box on floor U.L. legs
Plate of cookies/crackers
Empty bowl of popcorn
Blue bowl of fake ice and 4 labeled water bottles
Small bowl of Hershey's kisses
Bag of popcorn in brown shopping bag U.S.
Stool D.R.
Daily News on stool
Oscar's work gloves on table
3 clothes near gloves
4 stacked $1/_2$ apple boxes U.L. of table
Apple box on side S.L. of stack
Large apple box S.L. of table

OFF UPSTAGE RIGHT
Palm Pilot with stylus
Stainless-steel coffee mug
Bid fax
Pad folio
Stopwatch
Cell phone
Pen/pencil in pad folio
RON'S RIG:
> Cable coiled on rear hook (no slack)
> Power cord draped over rod twice
> Fresh white tape on coupling
> Glob of butyl
> Motor with controls facing D.
> Motor control — off
> No butyl on turntable
> Water pitcher withwater
> Cups
> Kleenex

RON'S BAG:
> Salt shaker in Ron's bag
> Ron's jean jacket on bag
> Turntable box

DRESSING ROOMS
RON'S TOOLBELT:
Polaroid
> Q-tip
> Gerber multipliers in nylon case
> Grease pencil
> Scissors
> Gloves
> Cloth
> Tin of butyl $3/4$ full
> Pair of white camera gloves

Extra Q-tips and thumbtacks for Ron
Jeffrey's keys

Jeffrey's phone
Jeffrey's coat
Dave's coat

DOWNSTAGE RIGHT
Large screen TV — volume down

SOUND EFFECTS

Loud, annoying whine of photosonics camera
Buzz of intercom

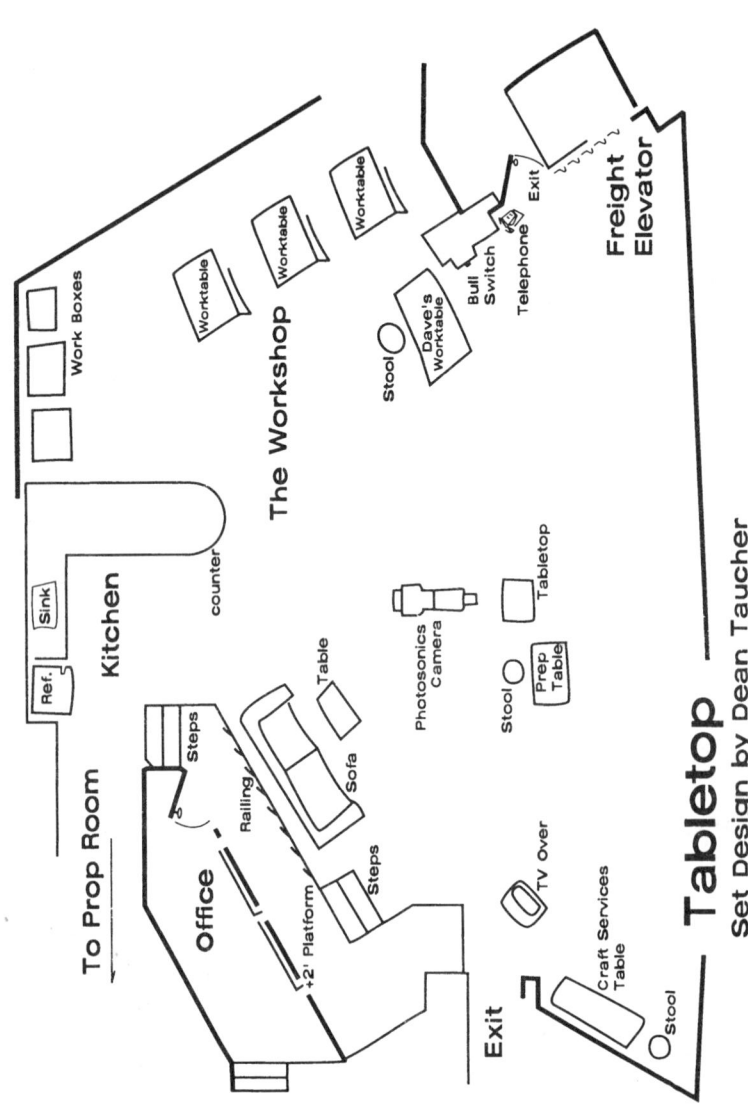

Tabletop
Set Design by Dean Taucher

To Prop Room

Work Boxes

Ref. Sink

Kitchen

counter

The Workshop

Worktable
Worktable
Worktable
Worktable

Stool
Dave's Worktable

Bull Switch

Telephone

Exit

Freight Elevator

Office

Steps
Railling
+2' Platform
Steps

Sofa
Table

Photosonics Camera

Stool
Prep Table
Tabletop

TV over

Craft Services Table

Stool

Exit